Physical Characteristics
of the Whippet
(from the American Kennel Club breed standard)

Back: Broad, firm and well muscled, having length over the loin.

Tail: Long and tapering, reaching to the hipbone when drawn through between the hind legs.

Hindquarters: Long and powerful. The thighs are broad and muscular, stifles well bent; muscles are long and flat and carry well down toward the hock. The hocks are well let down and close to the ground.

Size: Ideal height for dogs, 19 to 22 inches; for bitches, 18 to 21 inches, measured at the highest point of the withers.

Coat: Short, close, smooth and firm in texture.

Feet: Well formed with hard, thick pads. Toes should be long, close and well arched.

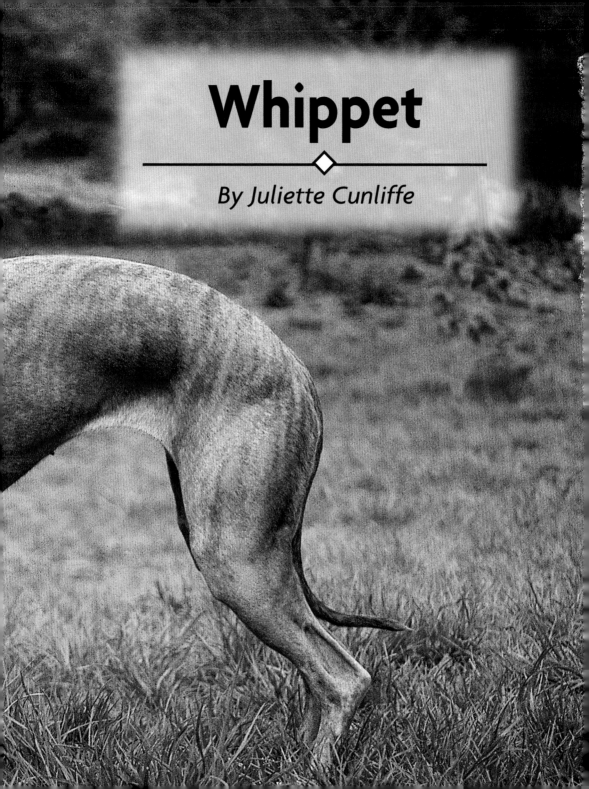

Whippet

◇

By Juliette Cunliffe

Contents

Training Your Whippet **84**

Begin with the basics of training the puppy and adult dog. Learn the principles of house-training the Whippet, including the use of crates and basic scent instincts. Enter Puppy Kindergarten and introduce the pup to his collar and leash, and progress to the basic commands. Find out about obedience classes and other activities.

Healthcare of Your Whippet **113**

By Lowell Ackerman DVM, DACVD
Become your dog's healthcare advocate and a well-educated canine keeper. Select a skilled and able veterinarian. Discuss pet insurance, vaccinations and infectious diseases, the neuter/spay decision and a sensible, effective plan for parasite control, including fleas, ticks and worms.

Your Senior Whippet **142**

Know when to consider your Whippet a senior and what special needs he will have. Learn to recognize the signs of aging in terms of physical and behavioral traits and what your vet can do to optimize your dog's golden years.

Showing Your Whippet **148**

Step into the center ring and find out about the world of showing pure-bred dogs. Here are the basics of how to get started in AKC shows and what's required for your dog to become a champion. Take a leap into the realms of obedience trials, agility, tracking and sighthound events.

KENNEL CLUB BOOKS: WHIPPET
ISBN: 1-59378-247-0

Copyright © 2005 • Kennel Club Books, LLC
308 Main Street, Allenhurst, New Jersey 07711 USA
Cover Design Patented: US 6,435,559 B2 • Printed in South Korea

Photography by Carol Ann Johnson
with additional photographs by

Big Paw Prints, Paulette Braun, T.J. Calhoun, Carolina Biological Supply, Juliette Cunliffe, Isabelle Français, Bill Jonas, Dr. Dennis Kunkel, Tam C. Nguyen, Phototake, Jean Claude Revy, Kent Standerford and Alice van Kempen.

Illustrations by Renée Low and Patricia Peters.

WHIPPET

EARLY SIGHTHOUND ANCESTORS AND DEVELOPMENT

The Whippet is one of a number of breeds that fall into the group of dogs classified as sighthounds, often known as gazehounds. These are hounds that hunt their prey largely by sight; their bodies are lean and powerful, with deep chests and long limbs providing both stamina and speed.

Such hounds are, in general, adapted for finding prey in open country. Once the prey has been located, it can be overtaken by speed and endurance. Because of this special form of hunting, sighthounds have historically been found in regions where there is open countryside, in North Africa, the Arab countries, Afghanistan, Russia, Ireland and Scotland. The modern Whippet, however, is a more recent member of this highly prized group of dogs and was developed by the miners and mill-hands of the north of England. It was often referred to as "the poor man's greyhound," a breed developed for rabbit coursing that later became involved in track racing.

The Asiatic Wolf is most commonly accepted as ancestor of the sighthounds, for no other wolves are known to have existed in areas where dogs of Greyhound type originated. Although the Whippet is considered a comparatively modern breed, it is worthy of note that the Greeks and Romans used small Greyhounds, these considerably smaller than the breed we know today.

In developing the Whippet, breeders aimed to create a dog that was like a small, fleet Greyhound, but it needed to be hardier than the small Italian Greyhound to succeed at its intended function of chasing and capturing

Illustration of the well-known Whippet Eng. Ch. Enterprise, published in 1900.

OPPOSITE PAGE: An elegant gazehound, the Whippet has been called "the poor man's greyhound," yet anyone who has known the virtues of a Whippet is rich indeed.

The Manchester Terrier is believed to have been used in the development of the Whippet, likely contributing its sleek coat and terrier pluck. A Toy Manchester adult and puppy are shown here.

FOOT AND FEATHER
A famous racing pigeon was once matched against a Whippet over a distance of 100 yards. The match included the rule that neither competitor was to rise more than six feet above the ground!

small game. Indeed the Whippet needed swiftness and grace as well as pluck and tenacity. With this in mind, several different breeds were involved in its creation. Certainly the Greyhound was used, as was the Italian Grey-

The Whippet was once called the "Hitalian," alluding to this ancestor, the Italian Greyhound.

hound, but there was also Airedale, Bedlington, Manchester, Yorkshire and English Terrier blood mixed in. This terrier blood could be seen in some of the long- or rough-coated dogs found during the early years of the breed's development.

Judicious breeding eventually produced a dog with the staying power of a working terrier combined with the speed and symmetry of the aristocratic sighthounds, its body shape having been gradually refined in harmony with that of the Greyhound. The Whippet we know and love so well today had been born.

In its early days, the Whippet was known by many different names, one of which was "Snap Dog," reputed to have arisen because, when running along a track or when meeting a strange dog, Whippets had a tendency to snap at one another. Another name by which the breed was known was "Hitalian," indicating the breed's Italian Greyhound origin.

It is said that the name "Whippet" may have been based on the word "whip," conveying the breed's sharp character and speed. Having said that, there was a breed called a "wappit," described briefly in the early decades of the nineteenth century. Today's Whippet may indeed have some connection with this breed.

ESTABLISHING A FOOTHOLD
Whippets were first classified as a breed in England at a show in Darlington in 1876, but the breed was not recognized by England's Kennel Club until 1890. The first five Whippets were registered in The Kennel Club's Stud Book the following year. Five was, though, a disappointing number, for it indicated that few owners were interested in actually registering their dogs, considering it a waste of both time and expense. In 1896, the breed was awarded Challenge Certificate (CC) status, meaning that the breed could earn championships, leading to what has become today one of the most numerically strong breeds on the British show scene. The breed's

The Italian Greyhound contributed its rainbow of coat colors and its rose-shaped ears to the Whippet.

first champion in Britain was Zuber, who claimed this prestigious title at The Kennel Club Show in October 1896, his first CCs having been awarded at Bath in 1894 and at Crystal Palace in 1895. Eng. Ch. Zuber was a highly influential sire, as indeed was his son, Eng. Ch. Enterprise. The first bitch to gain her crown was Eng. Ch. Manorley Model, this at The Kennel Club Show in 1897.

The Whippet's arch over its loin and superior ratting ability derive from this dog, the Bedlington Terrier.

WHIPPETS' DIETS
Quality meat was usually fed to Whippets just for the last few days prior to a race. More usually they ate a basin of broken bread, gravy and pudding, with tea and ale—essentially the same fare as that eaten by the family. Stories of Whippets being fed on bantams' eggs and old sherry are largely figments of the imagination!

In the late 1800s, Whippet racing was a sport of the lower classes in England. The stage of the race called "making ready" is shown above and below. The dogs are thrown into the race, as shown in the photo below. A pistol shot starts the race.

In 1899, Britain's Whippet Club was formed, aided to a large extent by that notable dog lady the Duchess of Newcastle. She was known primarily for her Borzoi and Fox Terriers, but she also exhibited the occasional Whippet and was a dedicated supporter of the breed. With the formation of a breed club, Kennel Club registrations rose significantly, but understandably during the troubled years of World War I, they declined again, with none registered in 1918.

There were many prominent and influential early kennels, some of which had been set up even before the turn of the century. Again, though, during World War II, many kennels fell into decline or were completely disbanded. There was a shortage of food, which inevitably had a drastic effect on the breeding and rearing of dogs of all breeds. A few breeders managed to keep their lines going through the war years and registrations once again increased as the 1940s progressed, with over 700 new registrations in 1947. In the 1960s, registrations surged, which is not always a good thing for a breed, but Whippet enthusiasts are thankfully a dedicated pack, keeping close tabs on breed soundness as numbers rose. In the last decade of the twentieth century, British registrations remained stable with between 1,431 and 1,747 Whippets registered annually, the latter figure a slight peak in 1996, although numbers subsequently dropped by a hundred or so.

In 1999, the Whippet Club celebrated its centenary year, holding an enormously well-supported show over a two-day period and encompassing all aspects of "Whippetdom," including obedience training, agility and lure coursing. The dog created primarily by the mining hands of northern England, often described as "a piece of canine art," is

A most famous Whippet is this Australian specimen known as Barna. It was owned by Joseph Brann and was the winner of the highest aggregate awarded by the Melbourne Metropolitan Kennel Club as well as many Whippet races.

indeed a breed of which to be proud.

THE WHIPPET IN TRACK RACING

In the nineteenth and early-twentieth century, dog racing was considered a "working-class sport" in the UK. Because of this, more wealthy enthusiasts did not participate easily in the free and easy atmosphere that surrounded it. Although the Ladies Kennel Association held a Whippet race, honored by the presence of King Edward and Queen Alexandra, this did not meet with the success that was hoped for.

Whippets used for both the track and for rabbit coursing needed to turn quickly and to be neat in using their head and teeth. It also was essential that they were capable of good speed. Those destined only for the track needed the power to get off quickly and, without interfering with the other runners, they had to move at speed to the end of the track.

The Greyhound closely resembles his relative, the Whippet, but is considerably larger, standing as tall as 30 inches or more at the shoulder.

Dogs frequently fought one another on the track and, on some tracks, canvas or nets were used to divide the lanes so as to prevent this problem. On other tracks, only string was used as a divider. A handicapping scale was used at most championship events, with divisions usually as follows: dogs over 23 lb., 23–18 lb., 18–12 lb.

WORLDLY WHIPPET

Whippets have made their mark in many countries throughout the world. In 1980, Ch. Beseeka Knight Errant of Silkstone won the award of Supreme Champion at the World Dog Show, a highly prestigious event held by the Fédération Cynologique Internationale in a different member country each year.

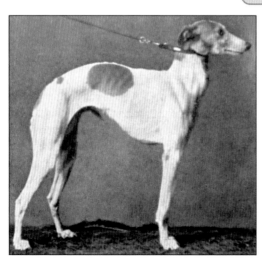

The Shirley prefix was very valued in Whippet circles during the 1930s. This photo depicts Mr. J. J. Holgate's Shirley Dixie.

and under 11 lb. In 1888, White Eye, a black dog with one white eye, held the world record for 21-lb dogs, covering 200 yards in 12 seconds. Descriptions of these relatively early races are thoroughly informative with intriguing snippets of information, such as that the jump of an 18-lb dog could exceed 15 feet.

Much time, trouble and money were expended in getting a Whippet into the peak of condition for the track, for heavy betting took place so that efforts could prove worthwhile. Lancashire, in the north of England, was considered the home of Whippet racing, and dogs from that county were thought to be of greater importance than those from elsewhere. Cinder tracks were faster than grass ones, and some

The famed Lottie Hampton, owned by Mr. W. Proctor, was greatly valued but did not have a successful show career.

BREED CLUBS
A great many countries have Whippet breed clubs, such as South Africa's Whippet Club of Transvaal, founded in 1984. The Whippet Club of Canada was not founded until 1993, but before then there were several regional Whippet clubs in the country and there are plenty of Whippet specialty shows there.

tracks in Lancashire were known throughout the world.

At the starting line, each dog was held by the tail and the scruff of the neck. Hearing the starting pistol, the slipper would swing his dog forward and throw the dog as far as he could, hoping he would land on his feet. Clearly a good

A famous British Whippet known as Eng. Ch. Zanza Zanita was born in 1931 and died in 1933. During her very brief life, she won her championship and many other prizes, including the three cups shown. She represented the best of her time.

Another of Mr. W. Proctor's popular dogs was the Whippet known as Eng. Ch. Manorley Model.

slipper gave the dog a great advantage! There was much shouting and yelling from onlookers, while at the other end of the track the dogs' owners shouted to their dogs, waving something at which their dog was to aim. That "something" was usually a piece of material or a towel, but it was sometimes a dead rabbit or even a pigeon.

Will O' The Wisp of Mimosaland, bred by Mr. W. L. Beard and owned by Mr. Douglas Todd, was considered one of the very best Whippets of the 1930s, a dog that conformed closely to the standard of the time.

EARLY TRAINING OF RACING WHIPPETS

To train young Whippets, puppies were called to their food by waving a rag, setting the scene for when they were older. Once they had grown, roadwork could be

Mixed Fortune, an extremely typical British Whippet whose show career was very successful, was owned and exhibited by Mr. Arthur Honeybone.

between 12 and 20 miles each day, with the aim of perfecting feet and muscle tone. For strenuous exercise, a ball was used.

Many Whippets were said to have eaten better food than their owners. Some of the best dogs were fed only on Scotch beef, sent down from Scotland especially for them because the local beef was not believed sufficiently good. Diet was carefully controlled, and some dogs were muzzled so that they were prevented from eating food not intended for them. Many

were kept almost entirely in the dark except when being raced, and they were fed and attended to by only one person, thus depriving them of what today would be considered essential companionship. In other respects, these highly prized dogs were treated with kindness, but standards of canine care then were not as they are today.

A successful dog was always the center of love and affection in the family, and often a family was actually supported by the winnings of the dog. Many unsuccessful dogs did not live out their natural lives, for poor men could not afford to keep bad stock. On the other hand, a good dog, too old for racing, often lived the rest of his life by the family fire.

Two portraits of Zanza Zanita, photographed by two different photographers.

LEFT, TOP: A New Zealand Whippet named Bonny Argyle was a top winner. LEFT, BOTTOM: Sandbloom was a beloved pet for Miss Robinson, representing a "pet-quality" dog from the early years.

TRICKS OF THE TRACK

Because money was involved in Whippet racing, a number of tricks were practiced regularly. Often a dog from another district was known by name, but not by sight, so a good dog could find itself entered under the name of an inferior one, playing havoc with the handicap system! An aid to those involved in such misdemeanors was that the dogs were kept under control until the moment the race commenced, so with skill even color could be

A scene from the turn of the century of a weigh-in prior to a Whippet race in England. Various races had weight standards because weight/height ratios impacted on stride lengths.

changed and the deed concealed. There was even a case of a dog being entered as a bitch!

Sometimes "holding" was employed, so that a dog was not slipped immediately at the sound of the gun. In fact, it was known for the pistol to go off and not one of the Whippets to be released from the slips. This was because each man slipping was betting on another's dog. It was by no means unknown for a dog to have one of its feet trodden to cause lameness. Even schoolchildren had a vested interest in the sport, for they were frequently quizzed by their teachers about which dogs would win.

Assessing the Whippet's gait in the show ring determines the relative soundness of the overall animal. Although a Whippet doesn't come close to full speed in the show ring, his gait should demonstrate that he is built for speed.

WHIPPETS IN AMERICA

In America the Whippet was recognized in 1888, first being seen in New England. A white dog with brown and yellow markings named Jack Dempsey was registered in the American Kennel Club's (AKC's) Stud Book that same year under the "Miscellaneous" heading. A bitch by the name of Boston Model was the first Whippet known to have won well at a dog show, taking first prize in a mixed breed class in 1893. Of course there have been many great kennels in America through the decades since then, the first of which was "Bay View," making its public appearance in the Whippet world in 1903. In 1904 Bay View Pride, whelped in 1902, became the first American champion.

Eight of America's first twelve Whippet champions came from the Bay View Kennels, which regularly entered exhibits at shows in the first ten years or so of the 1900s. The kennel was based in Rhode Island and also housed Greyhounds and hunting dogs. From 1912 onward, it seems no longer to have been active. The

This Whippet, Lady Beatrice, was bred by Mr. Boothe in Moose Jaw, Canada, in 1928. She was the first Whippet sent to Japan, where she became the prized possession of Miss A. Wada and a foundation of the Whippet in Japan.

The Standard Manchester Terrier, a Whippet relative, once excelled in a different kind of race: a contest of killing rats, of which the Manchester was an immodest winner.

Lansdown Kennels, owned by Ben Lewis, saw five Whippets carrying their championship titles before 1920, but they were not actually registered with the AKC. It must be said, though, that this frequently happened during that time period.

As the decades rolled along, so did the popularity of the Whippet, and several kennels produced a number of champions. There have been many big wins over the years, but an especially notewor-

Eng. Ch. Sparkle of Tytterton was owned by Mrs. Critchley Salmonson and was bred by K. Henley.

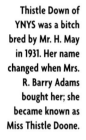

Thistle Down of YNYS was a bitch bred by Mr. H. May in 1931. Her name changed when Mrs. R. Barry Adams bought her; she became known as Miss Thistle Doone.

thy one was when the 12-year-old Ch. Hollypark Honey Bee took Best of Breed at the AKC Specialty Show in 1979, which takes some doing in any breed!

The only Whippet to win the famed Westminster Kennel Club Dog Show was Ch. Courtenay Fleetfoot of Pennyworth, owned by Pennyworth Kennels, in 1964. Surely one of the most famous American kennels in modern times is Sporting Fields, estab-

lished by Mr. and Mrs. James E. Butt in 1943 (originally with Poodles and Cockers). It was wonderful for the breed that the Butts took up Whippets in the early 1960s. Located in Tomsbrook, Virginia, Sporting Fields is currently owned and operated by

Brilliant Sand, a brindle bitch, won many first places in Open Shows and was owned by Mr. W. C. Taylor. Her beautiful clean body was exemplary of the breed in the early 1930s.

The Channel Islands champion was Mrs. W. J. de Gruchy's Memory Star. Among her many prizes was a Best in Show in 1934.

Butt's breeding program concentrates on breeding for both good temperament as well as well-rounded dogs. Surely Dual Ch. Sporting Fields Jazz Fest, the first dog to be ranked number-one in the show ring and in the field, and Dual Ch. Sporting Fields Winsome Won (the only Whippet to win Best in Show, Best in Field and Best in Specialty Show) attest to the success of the program, as does OTCh. Sporting Fields Mad Hatter, the first and only Whippet

their daughter Debbie Butt and continues its reputation as the nation's leading Whippet kennel with nearly 300 champions. Some of their famous Whippets include Ch. Sporting Fields Clansman and his great-grandson Am. Can. Ch. Sporting Fields Kinsman, each of whom was the winner of 59 Best in Show awards and sire of dozens of champions. Debbie

Born in July 1928, Silver Lightning was an exceptionally fast runner who won numerous prizes and sired many champions.

to earn this coveted obedience title. As Debbie's children are continuing with the kennel, Sporting Fields becomes one of the US's few prestigious third-generation breeding establishments.

In addition to Sporting Fields, there are other great names such as Starline and, of course, Bo Bengston's Bohem Kennel. This was originally established in Sweden over four decades ago and has to be one of the most

LEFT: Eng. Ch. Silver Knight was a fawn and white dog born in 1930. He was a consistent winner at the shows.

The antique collars worn by champion runners of yore are coming back into fashion for modern-day champions.

show benches but also in the sporting field.

Although Whippets at general shows usually enjoy greater popularity in Britain than in America, at breed specialty shows numbers exhibited have reached phenomenal figures—over 500 on occasions. It is interesting to note that the proportion of judges in America who are breed specialists is small in comparison with breed specialist judges at shows in the UK.

Within the AKC, the American Whippet Club (AWC) is the national club for the breed and promotes responsible ownership, ethical breeding as well as showing, obedience training and lure coursing. The AWC holds a national specialty each year in different parts of the country, and sponsors six regional Whippet specialties. The Club awards Registers of Merit and Awards of Versatility.

successful kennels in the world, especially given that relatively few litters are bred. Another notable kennel is Karasar, with interests lying not only on the

Flying Imp, owned by J. Cahill, celebrated his first birthday by winning the Napier Whippet Puppy Cup in Australia. He also won the Wellington Cup in the most important North Island race, running 200 yards in slightly over 12 seconds.

WHIPPETS IN AUSTRALIA

It is likely that even in the nineteenth century some settlers in Australia took their Whippets with them, and Whippet racing was certainly recorded in 1869. However, not until the twentieth century were Whippets bred specifically for the show ring.

British imported stock has had a great influence on the Whippet scene in Australia, in part because of quarantine laws in the UK, making it easier to import from

Britain than from elsewhere. Several Whippets have won high awards at prestigious shows here, one early such achievement being Ch. Calpin Bartic's Best in Show win at Brisbane Royal in 1951.

WHIPPETS IN EUROPE

In Scandinavia, Whippets were shown as long ago as 1900, and in about 1917 Queen Maude of Norway imported two Whippets to Norway, giving certain acceptability to the breed. As in other countries, many Scandinavian enthusiasts are seriously dedicated to their breed and the *Svenska Whipptklubben* (Swedish Whippet Club) was formed in 1976.

The Whippet scene elsewhere in Europe is somewhat different, France being the country in which the breed is most popular. A

Whippets excel in show rings today and are represented by strong entries. Not only is the number of dogs entered high but also the quality of the dogs is consistently impressive.

French breed club was formed in the late 1940s and the breed club shows attract substantial entries. However, although a goodly number of Whippets are registered in France each year, many of them are destined for pet homes rather than the show ring.

In Germany, Whippets were first registered in 1903 but in those early years there was not always a clear defining line between large Italian Greyhounds and Whippets. Until the war years, several British-bred Whippets were imported into Germany, but today the breed is not greatly popular there, with registration numbers being similar to those in Switzerland, despite the disparity in size and population between the two countries.

Whippets prove obedient and elegant in the show ring. This handler and Whippet are making a very professional showing.

CHARACTERISTICS OF THE

WHIPPET

Upon viewing this elegant creature, who could debate the Whippet's being described as "a piece of canine art"? Nothing is nearer to the truth. A well-constructed Whippet is a truly beautiful animal with grace displayed in every movement, whether speeding across a field, investigating the yard or reclining comfortably on the sofa or bed. The breed's graceful lines are clearly seen thanks to the smooth coat, making a feast for the eyes of any true lover of sighthounds.

The Whippet is a highly adaptable dog and can fit in well with most household situations. His size, short coat and clean habits make him easy to have around and a pleasure to keep.

PERSONALITY

The Whippet is a wonderful companion dog; this is an affectionate, gentle and faithful breed with an even temper and quiet disposition. The Whippet may give warning barks, but overall it is a quiet breed, not given to unnecessary barking. Whippets are very quick and, especially as youngsters, are quite capable of dashing off for some important purpose they have in mind (often connected with food). This means that an owner has to keep a careful eye on his Whippet's whereabouts and surroundings.

Whippets adore the company of those they know and most are all too happy to snuggle up on your lap when given the opportunity, even if you are sunning yourself in the yard in the heat of the day. Most Whippets do seem to be sun worshipers and undoubtedly enjoy both heat and comfort. There is also many a Whippet that sleeps under the covers on his owner's bed, providing warmth and companionship for those who allow it (and admit to it). It has to be said that a Whippet is rather like an animated hot-water bottle!

WHIPPETS AND OTHER PETS

Because of their nature, some Whippets do not take kindly to cats and other small creatures, so sensible management is prudent if introducing a Whippet to the family cat or vice versa. A Whippet must be taught to know the

WHIPPET ANCESTORS

Although considered a relatively new creation as a specific breed, dogs similar to those we know today as Whippets have been around for many a long year. In 1841, such dogs were described as "a dog bred betwixt a greyhound and a spaniel." But referring back to a dictionary of 1550, the word "whippet" was defined as "a lively young woman; a light wench."

rules of the household, and that does not involve chasing the family feline. Cats, though, seem to sense which dogs they need to respect and which they do not, which helps what might otherwise, perhaps, be a slightly difficult situation.

Of course, the majority of Whippets, if socialized carefully with other family pets from an early age, are able to live alongside them in perfect harmony. Many a Whippet and cat form firm friendships and become almost inseparable. However, even though your Whippet may have accepted the family cat, the same sentiment does not likely apply when a neighbor's cat has the audacity to venture into your yard!

WHIPPETS WITH CHILDREN

The parent of both dogs and children must teach the latter to

A living work of art, the Whippet is an elegant dog, seemingly aloof but actually a wonderful companion.

The author and her niece take their Whippet on long walks into the countryside.

respect their canine friends and to treat them gently. Whippets are tolerant dogs and most thoroughly enjoy the company of children, especially if they have been sensibly introduced while the dog is still young. Nonetheless, one should always keep in mind that Whippets, like all other dogs, appreciate some peace and quiet and that the limits of their tolerance should never be put to the test. Careful supervision is the key to building up a successful relationship between child and dog.

SIZE

Whippets might be considered of medium size, their height ranging between 18–22 inches, bitches being the smaller of the two sexes (as in most breeds). However, because of its fine construction this is not a heavy breed, so actual weight is considerably less than most other breeds that attain this height. This means that Whippets can be picked up with relative ease when necessary.

Adaptable and affectionate, Whippets enjoy the company of human and canine family members.

Because of their long legs, Whippets can not only move quickly but also have an ability to reach up to things that one might naively consider to be out of reach. Tasty morsels left on kitchen counters are by no means beyond their grasp, and it can be rather amusing to see a Whippet do a quick circuit of the kitchen, stretching up on his hind legs to see what might be available for the taking!

Sometimes a Whippet's long legs seem to stretch out endlessly when reclining, so one must take care not to sit on a Whippet accidentally, especially if the dog is concealed under some cozy item like a cushion or blanket.

LIFESPAN
Clearly, when taking a Whippet into your home, the ultimate aim will be that the dog remains with

Enjoying a rest in the sun, this Whippet has been alerted to a sharp sound.

You can count on your Whippet to be curious about his surroundings and alert to all going on around him.

SKIN, COAT AND COLOR

A Whippet's coat is fine, short and close in texture, so it can be kept easily under control with simple grooming and general care. The colors of this breed are many and varied, and there is no preference for any color. Therefore Whippets are found in a wide variety of hues, ranging from white through to black, with brindles and parti-colors mixed in for further variety. This array of colors is just another interesting aspect of this delightful breed. Of course, some people will have personal preferences regarding color, and in some breeding lines a particular color appears more frequently than others, but selection should certainly never be made on color alone.

The skin of the Whippet is fine and, since it is without the protection of a long coat, can mark and tear rather easily. This should be kept in mind when selecting areas for a Whippet's free run; low branches and the like can be damaging.

HEALTH CONSIDERATIONS

Although basically a healthy breed, every breed is prone to certain problems, and some Whippets do suffer from illnesses. It is only fair to owners and to the dogs in question that attention is brought to these illnesses. Awareness of any prob-

you for life. A healthy Whippet can be expected to live on average for around 14 years, but many enjoy even longer lives. It is not at all unusual to come across some moderately sprightly Whippets at 16 years of age.

WEIGHING WHIPPETS

The easiest method of weighing your Whippet is on the bathroom scale. First weigh yourself alone, then a second time while holding the dog in your arms. Deduct one from the other to obtain the accurate weight of your hound.

Whippet sleeps in the house be away from drafts, so the crate or bed should be raised slightly off the ground.

OBESITY

Most Whippets love their food and may well put on excess weight, especially as they progress toward old age. All

lems that may possibly arise can help owners to know when it is necessary to seek veterinary advice.

ANESTHESIA SENSITIVITY

Whippets, like other sighthounds, have a very low proportion of body fat in relation to their size. As a result, anesthesia is one of various medications to which Whippets are sensitive, so it is important to discuss this with your veterinarian prior to any surgery. A special anesthetic that is more suitable for the Whippet and similar breeds can be used, and it is recommended that barbiturates be avoided.

FEELING THE COLD

In part because of their thin skin and their low proportion of body fat, Whippets do feel the cold more than many other dogs. They need to wear warm doggie sweaters when outside in cold weather. They also seem rather susceptible to cold winds. It is also important that where the

"I found a Whippet in my bed when I awoke!" Properly socialized, Whippets are great companions for children.

"I'm ready to come back in!" Whippets cannot tolerate the cold, preferring to be indoors in wintry weather.

Whippets enjoy being with their owners at all times. They are very devoted pets.

Whippets, especially older ones, should always be kept trim. There are really no adequate excuses for not noticing that your Whippet is putting on weight. It's easy to see every extra pound on this breed, even without a scale.

Given the choice, Whippets prefer to cuddle up with their loved ones when it's time to relax.

DENTAL HEALTH

Although Whippets usually have strong teeth, it is always important to pay close attention to the care of teeth and gums. That way, they will remain as healthy as possible with consequent prevention of decay, infection and resultant loss of teeth.

Infection in the gums may not just stop there. The bacteria

from such infection is carried through the bloodstream, the result of which can be diseases of the liver, kidney, heart and joints. This is all the more reason to realize that efficient dental care is of utmost importance throughout any dog's life.

SUNBURN

Because Whippets love the sun so much, care should be taken that the sun does not burn their rather delicate skin, especially on the muzzle. A little gentle sun cream can be applied on the muzzles of Whippets who really do insist on lying outside too long. Obviously owners should encourage their dogs to go inside the house or to a shady spot for cooling off from time to time, and it is easy to tell when they are really getting too hot, because they pant visibly.

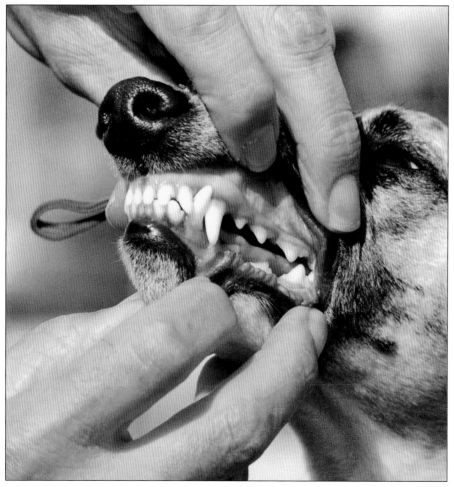

Whippets have strong teeth but their health should be monitored regularly. Brush your Whippet's teeth at least once a week and check his mouth regularly; the vet will give a thorough dental exam at your Whippet's regular checkups.

BREED STANDARD FOR THE

WHIPPET

The official breed standard for the Whippet is effectively a "blueprint" for the breed. It sets down the various points of the dog in words, enabling a visual picture to be conjured up in the mind of the reader. However, this is more easily said than done. Not only do standards vary from country to country, but people's interpreta-

How each dog measures up in the show ring is based on the breed standard, the blueprint of the ideal Whippet.

tions of breed standards vary also. It is this difference of interpretation that makes judges select different dogs for top honors, for their opinions differ as to which dog most closely fits the breed standard. That is not to say that a good dog does not win regularly under different judges, nor that an inferior dog may rarely even be placed at a show, at least not among quality competition.

An example of a difference among standards is that of the height specifications in the US and UK standard. The AKC's specifications for height are: dogs, 19–22 inches (48–56 cm), and bitches, 18–21 inches (46–53 cm), both sexes being allowed greater height in the US than in England. The UK allows 18.5–20 inches for dogs and 17.5–18.5 inches for bitches. The AKC standard states that Whippets that are more than half an inch below or above the stipulated heights are disqualified.

Because of the Whippet's delicate skin, it is not uncommon for dogs in show rings throughout the world to exhibit scars, and I hope no understanding judges penalize these. The AKC standard goes so far as to say, "Old scars and injuries, the result of work or accident, should not be allowed to prejudice the dog's chance in the show ring."

Although one could discuss the differences between these and the standards of other countries for many more pages than the text of this book will allow, it is time to move on to the official standard. The breed standard given here in full is that approved by the American Kennel Club. It is rather comprehensive and is fairly self-explanatory, written by the American Whippet Club.

THE AMERICAN KENNEL CLUB STANDARD FOR THE WHIPPET

General Appearance: A medium-size sighthound giving the appearance of elegance and fitness, denoting great speed, power and balance without coarseness. A true sporting hound that covers a maximum of distance with a minimum of lost motion. Should convey an impression of beautifully balanced muscular power and strength, combined with great elegance and grace of outline. Symmetry of outline, muscular development and powerful gait are the main considerations; the dog being built for speed and work, all forms of exaggeration should be avoided.

Size, Proportion, Substance: Ideal height for dogs, 19 to 22 inches; for bitches, 18 to 21 inches, measured at the highest point of the withers. More than one-half inch above or below the stated limits will disqualify. Length from forechest to buttocks equal to or slightly greater than height at the withers. Moderate bone throughout.

Head: Keen intelligent alert expression. Eyes large and dark. Both eyes must be of the same color. Yellow or light eyes should be strictly penalized. Blue or wall eyes shall disqualify. Fully pigmented eyelids are desirable.

The judge at a dog show determines how well your Whippet conforms to the breed standard. The dog that most closely conforms is deemed Best of Breed.

Rose *ears*, small, fine in texture; in repose, thrown back and folded along neck. Fold should be maintained when at attention. Erect ears should be severely penalized. *Skull* long and lean, fairly wide between the ears, scarcely perceptible stop. *Muzzle* should be long and powerful, denoting great strength of bite, without coarseness. Lack of underjaw should be strictly penalized. Nose entirely black. *Teeth* of upper jaw should fit closely over teeth of lower jaw creating a scissors bite. Teeth should be white and strong. Undershot shall disqualify. Overshot one-quarter inch or more shall disqualify.

Neck, Topline, Body: Neck long, clean and muscular, well arched with no suggestion of throatiness, widening gracefully into the top of the shoulder. A short thick neck, or a ewe neck, should be penalized. The *back* is broad, firm and well muscled, having length

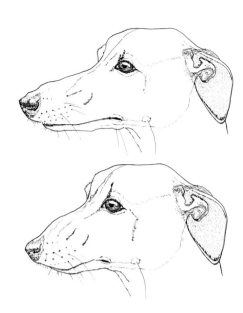

The top figure illustrates a Whippet with a correct muzzle. The lower figure illustrates a Whippet with a muzzle that is too short.

The Whippet's outline is marked by grace and elegance.

over the loin. The backline runs smoothly from the withers with a graceful natural arch, not too accentuated, beginning over the loin and carrying through over the croup; the arch is continuous without flatness. A dip behind shoulder blades, wheelback, flat back, or a steep or flat croup should be penalized. *Brisket* very deep, reaching as nearly as possible to the point of the elbow. Ribs well sprung but with no suggestion of barrel shape. The space between the forelegs is filled in so that there is no appearance of a hollow between them. There is a definite tuckup of the underline.

Correct body type: deep chest and long, strong back.

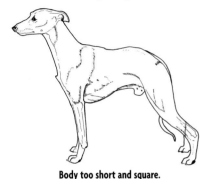

Body too short and square.

The *tail* long and tapering, reaching to the hipbone when drawn through between the hind legs. When the dog is in motion, the tail is carried low with only a gentle upward curve; tail should not be carried higher than top of back.

Forequarters: *Shoulder blade* long, well laid back, with flat muscles, allowing for moderate space between shoulder blades at peak of withers. Upper arm of equal length, placed so that the elbow falls directly under the withers. The points of the elbows should point neither in nor out, but straight back. A steep shoulder, short upper arm, a heavily muscled or loaded shoulder, or a very narrow shoulder, all of which restrict low free movement, should be strictly penalized. *Forelegs* straight, giving appearance of strength and substance of bone. Pasterns strong, slightly bent and flexible. Bowed legs, tied-in elbows, legs lacking substance, legs set far under the body so as to create an exaggerated forechest, weak or upright pasterns should be strictly penalized. Both front and rear feet must be well formed with hard, thick pads. Feet more hare than cat, but both are acceptable. Flat, splayed or soft feet without thick hard pads should be strictly penalized. Toes should be long, close and well arched. Nails strong and naturally short or of moderate length. Dewclaws may be removed.

Hindquarters: Long and powerful. The thighs are broad and muscular, stifles well bent; muscles are long and flat and carry well down toward the hock. The hocks are well let down and close to the ground. Sickle or cow hocks should be strictly penalized.

Coat: Short, close, smooth and firm in texture. Any other coat

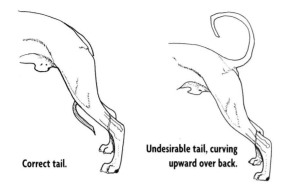

Correct tail.

Undesirable tail, curving upward over back.

shall be a disqualification. Old scars and injuries, the result of work or accident, should not be allowed to prejudice the dog's chance in the show ring.

Color: Color immaterial.

Gait: Low, free moving and smooth, with reach in the forequarters and strong drive in the hindquarters. The dog has great freedom of action when viewed from the side; the forelegs move forward close to the ground to give a long, low reach; the hind legs have strong propelling power. When moving and viewed from front or rear, legs should turn neither in nor out, nor should feet cross or interfere with each other. Lack of front reach or rear drive, or a short, hackney gait with high wrist action, should be strictly penalized. Crossing in front or moving too close should be strictly penalized.

Temperament: Amiable, friendly, gentle, but capable of great intensity during sporting pursuits.

Disqualifications: *More than one-half inch above or below stated height limits. Blue or wall eyes. Undershot, overshot one-quarter inch or more. Any coat other than short, close, smooth and firm in texture.*

Approved August 10, 1993
Effective September 29, 1993

COMMENTS ON THE STANDARD
Although a great deal can be learned from the breed standard, only by seeing good-quality, typical specimens can one really learn to appreciate the breed's merits. Therefore readers interested in showing their Whippets should watch other dogs being exhibited and learn as much as possible from established breeders and exhibitors. Personally, I have found Whippet exhibitors to be a

Figure on left shows correct forequarters. Figure on right illustrates a dog that is too broad in front.

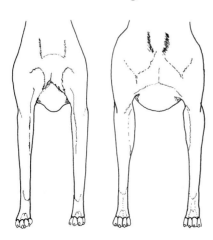

most helpful and dedicated bunch of people, so undoubtedly there are many people out there who are willing to give advice and assistance to a newcomer.

It is helpful to attend breed seminars when available. Here the finer points of the breed can be explained fully and discussed. There is usually a dog, or perhaps a handful, available for demonstration purposes, and there may be an opportunity for participants to gain hands-on experience, giving a valuable insight into the structure of the animal.

The Whippet is a breed built both for speed and for work, and good-quality specimens should easily portray this. They need to be well muscled, but that muscle should be hard and flat, not overly bulging as is more appropriate for some heavier breeds.

Because of the Whippet's work as a hunting dog, the neck is important. We can see from the standard that the neck is to be long, muscular and arched. A Whippet with a long neck must, of necessity, have correct shoulder layback, without which the head can simply not be carried as it should. Faults in shoulder construction also play havoc with movement, as do so many other important aspects of a dog's physical makeup.

It would be all too easy to take each part of the beautiful Whippet and explain in depth why it

A proud Junior Handler shows off her well-trained Whippet.

should be as it is, but that would be a book in itself! However, it must be brought to your attention that the chest is to be deep and the ribs well sprung, thus allowing sufficient heart room; this is a breed that needs both heart and lung capacity for the breed's intended function in life.

Although there is an arch over the loin, this, like the rest of the dog, should not be exaggerated and therefore should not form a hump as is occasionally seen. The outline of the Whippet is one that flows gracefully. Again, because of the breed's function, it must be capable of driving from the hindquarters; the proper construction is well described in the standard.

The Whippet is a breed of great beauty, combining muscular power, strength, elegance and grace, and should be unexaggerated in any way. Long may it remain thus!

WHIPPET

You probably decided on a Whippet as your choice of pet following a visit to the home of a friend or acquaintance, where you saw a graceful Whippet wandering quietly around the house and relaxing in his favorite spots. However, as a potential new owner, you must realize that a good deal of care, commitment and careful training goes into raising a boisterous puppy so that your pet turns into a well-behaved adult such as this. In deciding to take on a new puppy, you will be committing yourself to around 14 years of responsibility. No dog

should be discarded after a few months, or even a few years, after the novelty has worn off. Instead, your Whippet should be joining your household to spend the rest of his days with you.

Although temperamentally a Whippet is fairly easy to look after, you will still need to carry out a certain amount of training. You need to be firm so that your dog knows exactly who is in control. However, to produce the most effective results, training should not be not overly strict.

A Whippet generally likes to be clean around the house, but you will need to teach your

THE FAMILY TREE

Your puppy's pedigree is his family tree. Just as a child may resemble his parents and grandparents, so too will a puppy reflect the qualities, good and bad, of his ancestors, especially those in the first two generations. Therefore, it's important to know as much as possible about a puppy's immediate relatives. Reputable and experienced breeders should be able to explain the pedigree and why they chose to breed from the particular dogs they used.

puppy what is and what is not acceptable. You will need to be consistent in your instructions; it is no good allowing certain behavior one day and not the next. Not only will your puppy simply not understand, he will be utterly confused. Your Whippet will want to please you, so you will need to demonstrate clearly to your puppy how he is to achieve this.

The dog you are taking into your home will grow up to be medium in size but will have what sometimes appear to be extraordinarily long legs. These, coupled with a long neck, long muzzle and keen eyesight, provide an opportunity for plenty of mischief if your Whippet sees

Adding a Whippet to your life means the companionship of a wonderful canine friend for well over a decade.

A SHOW PUPPY

If you plan to show your puppy, you must first deal with a reputable breeder who shows his dogs and has had some success in the conformation ring. The puppy's pedigree should include one or more champions in the first and second generation. You should be familiar with the breed and breed standard so you can know what qualities to look for in your puppy. The breeder's observations and recommendations also are invaluable aids in selecting your future champion. If you consider an older puppy, be sure that the puppy has been properly socialized with people and not isolated in a kennel without substantial daily human contact.

fit! You may wish to consider erecting baby gates so that your new hound is restricted to certain areas of the house. That will work at least for the time being, although your Whippet may soon learn to jump them as he grows! There will undoubtedly be a period of training and settling in, a period during which you may have needed to rearrange some of your household items so that nothing will cause injury or get broken.

Whatever the problems encountered, this will be a period of great fun, but you must be prepared for mishaps around the home during the first few weeks of your lives together. It will be important that breakable items are kept well out of harm's way, and you will have to think twice about where you place hot cups of coffee or anything else that could cause harm if knocked over. Accidents can and do happen, so you will need to think ahead to prevent them. Electric cables must

Believe it or not, puppies aren't "on the go" all of the time! They need lots of time to rest, too.

be carefully concealed, and your puppy must be taught where he can and cannot go.

Before making your commitment to a new puppy, do also think carefully about your future vacation plans. Will you want your dog to travel with you? If not, do you have a suitable option for his care while you are away? If you have thought all of these things through carefully and discussed the matter thoroughly with all family members, you should have come to the right decision. If you decide that a Whippet will join your family, this will hopefully be a happy long-term relationship for all parties concerned.

The love of the race is a natural instinct for Whippet puppies. New owners are advised to limit vigorous "horse play" until their Whippets have developed their limbs completely.

BUYING A WHIPPET PUPPY
Although you may be looking for a Whippet as a pet, rather than a show dog, this does not mean that you want a dog that is in any way

"second-rate." A caring breeder will have brought up the entire litter of puppies with the same amount of dedication, and a puppy destined for a pet home

should be just as healthy as one that hopes to end up in the show ring or on the race track.

Because you have carefully selected this breed, you will want a Whippet that is a typical specimen, in both looks and temperament. In your endeavors to find such a puppy, you will have to select the breeder with care. The American Kennel Club and the American Whippet Club are trusted sources for breeder referrals and information on breed clubs in your region. Through a nearby breed club, you can probably be put in touch with breeders.

MATERNAL MOOD
When selecting a puppy, be certain to meet the dam of the litter. The temperament of the dam is often predictive of the temperament of her puppies. However, dams occasionally are very protective of their young, some to the point of being testy or aggressive with visitors, whom they may view as a danger to their babies. Such attitudes are more common when the pups are very young and still nursing and should not be mistaken for actual aggressive temperament. If possible, visit the dam away from her pups to make friends with her and gain a better understanding of her true personality.

To obtain a pup from the breeder of your choice, you may have to be put on a waiting list, but it is better to wait for quality than to make a hurried decision. It is important that you have done your homework carefully, so that you feel both breed and breeder are right for you.

Even though you are probably not looking for a show dog, it is always a good idea to visit a show so that you can see quality specimens of the breed. This will also give you an opportunity to meet owners and handlers who will probably be able to answer some of your queries. In addition, you will get some idea about which breeders' lines you prefer by seeing the dogs in action.

When buying your puppy, you will need to know about vaccinations, those already given and

those due. It is important that any injections already given by a veterinarian have documentation to prove this. A worming routine is also vital for any young puppy, so the breeder should be able to tell you exactly what treatment has been given, when it has been administered and how you should continue.

Clearly when selecting a puppy, the one you choose must be in good condition. The coat should look healthy and there should be no discharge from eyes or nose. Ears should also be clean, and of course there should be absolutely no sign of parasites. Check that there is no rash on the skin, and of course the puppy you choose should not have evidence of loose stools.

Finally, a few words of advice. Always insist that you see the puppy's dam and, if possible, the sire. However, frequently the sire will not be owned by the breeder of the litter, but the breeder should have at least his photo and pedigree to show you. Ask if the breeder has any other of the puppy's relations that you could meet. For example, there may be an older half-sister or half-brother and it would be interesting for you to see how he/she has turned out in eventual size, overall quality, temperament and so on.

Be sure, too, that if you decide to buy a puppy, all relevant documentation is provided at the time

PUPPY IMMUNITY

Puppies are born with natural antibodies that protect them from most canine diseases. They receive more antibodies from the colostrum in their mother's milk. These immunities wear off, however, and must be replaced through a series of vaccines. Puppy shots are given at 3- to 4-week intervals starting at 6 to 8 weeks of age through 16 to 20 weeks of age. Booster shots are given after one year of age, and every one to three years thereafter.

of sale. You will need a copy of the pedigree, AKC registration documents, vaccination certificates and a feeding chart so that you know exactly how the puppy has been fed and how you should continue. Some careful breeders also provide their puppy buyers with a small amount of food. This prevents the risk of an upset tummy, allowing for a gradual change of diet if you choose to feed a different type of food.

A COMMITTED NEW OWNER

By now you should understand what makes the Whippet a most unique and special dog, one that may fit nicely into your family and lifestyle. If you have researched breeders, you should be able to recognize a knowledgeable and responsible Whippet

Even at a young age, a Whippet possesses the breed's expression of keen intelligence.

breeder who cares not only about his pups but also about what kind of owner you will be. If you have completed the final step in your new journey, you have found a litter, or possibly two, of quality Whippet pups.

A visit with the puppies and their breeder should be an education in itself. Breed research, breeder selection and puppy visitation are very important aspects of finding the puppy of your dreams. Beyond that, these things also lay the foundation for a successful future with your pup. Puppy personalities within each litter vary, from the shy and easy-going puppy to the one who is dominant and assertive, with most pups falling somewhere in between. By spending time with the puppies, you will be able to recognize certain behaviors and what these behaviors indicate about each pup's temperament.

> **MAKE A COMMITMENT**
>
> Dogs are most assuredly man's best friend, but they are also a lot of work. When you add a puppy to your family, you also are adding to your daily responsibilities for years to come. Dogs need more than just food, water and a place to sleep. They also require training (which can be ongoing throughout the lifetime of the dog), activity to keep them physically and mentally fit and hands-on attention every day, plus grooming and health care. Your life as you now know it may well disappear! Are you prepared for such drastic changes?

PEDIGREE VS. REGISTRATION CERTIFICATE

Too often new owners are confused between these two important documents. Your puppy's pedigree, essentially a family tree, is a written record of a dog's genealogy of three generations or more. The pedigree will show you the names as well as performance titles of all dogs in your pup's background. Your breeder must provide you with a registration application, with his part properly filled out. You must complete the application and send it to the AKC with the proper fee. Every puppy must come from a litter that has been AKC-registered by the breeder, born in the US and from a sire and dam that are also registered with the AKC.

The seller must provide you with complete records to identify the puppy. The AKC requires that the seller provide the buyer with the following: breed; sex, color and markings; date of birth; litter number (when available); names and registration numbers of the parents; breeder's name; and date sold or delivered.

Which type of pup will complement your family dynamics is best determined by observing the puppies in action within their "pack." Your breeder's expertise and recommendations are very valuable. Although you may fall in love with a bold and brassy male, the breeder may suggest that another pup would be best for you. The breeder's experience in rearing Whippet pups and matching their temperaments with appropriate humans offers the best assurance that your pup will meet your needs and expectations. The type of puppy that you select is just as important as your decision that the Whippet is the breed for you.

The decision to live with a Whippet is a serious commitment and not one to be taken lightly. This puppy is a living sentient being that will be dependent on you for basic survival for his entire life. Beyond the basics of survival—food, water, shelter and protection—he needs much, much more. The new pup needs love, nurturing and a proper canine education to mold him into a responsible, well-behaved canine citizen. Your Whippet's health and good manners will need consistent monitoring and regular "tune-ups," so your job as a responsible

Raising a litter is hard work for mom and breeder.

COST OF OWNERSHIP

The purchase price of your puppy is merely the first expense in the typical dog budget. Quality dog food, veterinary care (sickness and health maintenance), dog supplies and grooming costs will add up to big bucks every year. Can you adequately afford to support a canine addition to the family?

dog owner will be ongoing throughout every stage of his life. If you are not prepared to accept these responsibilities and commit to them for the next decade, likely longer, then you are not prepared to own a dog of any breed.

Although the responsibilities of owning a dog may at times tax your patience, the joy of living with your Whippet far outweighs the workload, and a well-mannered adult dog is worth your time and effort. Before your eyes, your new charge will grow up to be your most loyal friend, devoted to you unconditionally.

YOUR WHIPPET SHOPPING LIST

Just as expectant parents prepare a nursery for their baby, so should you ready your home for the arrival of your Whippet pup. If you have the necessary puppy supplies purchased and in place before he comes home, it will ease the puppy's transition from the

These Whippet puppies are only a few days old. At this tender age, their eyes haven't even opened yet.

warmth and familiarity of his mom and littermates to the brand-new environment of his new home and human family. You will be too busy to stock up and prepare your house after your pup comes home, that's for sure! Imagine how a pup must feel upon being transported to a strange new place. It's up to you to comfort him and to let your little pup know that he is going to be happy with you.

FOOD AND WATER BOWLS

Your puppy will need separate bowls for his food and water. Stainless steel pans are generally preferred over plastic bowls since they sterilize better and pups are less inclined to chew on the metal. Heavy-duty ceramic bowls are popular, but consider how often you will have to pick up those

Your Whippet does not require very large bowls, but he does require sturdy bowls that are easy for you to clean but not easy for him to chew.

heavy bowls. Buy adult-sized pans, as your puppy will grow into them before you know it.

THE DOG CRATE

If you think that crates are tools of punishment and confinement for when a dog has misbehaved, think again. Most breeders and almost all trainers recommend a crate as the preferred house-training aid as well as for all-around puppy training and safety. Because dogs are natural den creatures that prefer cave-like environments, the benefits of crate use are many. The crate provides the puppy with his very own "safe house," a cozy place to sleep, take a break or seek comfort with a favorite toy; a travel aid to house your dog when on the road, at motels or at the vet's office; a

Wire crates are ideal for the active Whippet who always needs to see what's going on around him. The wire crate also provides the best ventilation.

> **CRATE EXPECTATIONS**
>
> To make the crate more inviting to your puppy, you can offer his first meal or two inside the crate, always keeping the crate door open so that he does not feel confined. Keep a favorite toy or two in the crate for him to play with while inside. You can also cover the crate at night with a lightweight sheet to make it more den-like and remove the stimuli of household activity. Never put him into his crate as punishment or as you are scolding him, since he will then associate his crate with negative situations and avoid going there.

training aid to help teach your puppy proper toileting habits; a place of solitude when non-dog people happen to drop by and don't want a lively puppy—or even a well-behaved adult dog—saying hello or begging for their attention.

Crates come in several types, although the wire crate and the fiberglass airline-type crate are the most common. Both are safe and your puppy will adjust to either

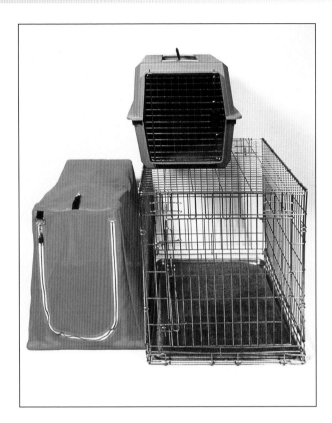

cases. However, a mesh crate might not be suitable for a pup with manic chewing habits.

Don't bother with a puppy-sized crate. Although your Whippet will be a wee fellow when you bring him home, he will grow up in the blink of an eye and your puppy crate will be useless. Purchase a crate that will accommodate an adult Whippet. A crate of 36 inches long by 24 inches wide by 28 inches high is recommended for the Whippet.

BEDDING AND CRATE PADS

Your puppy will enjoy some type of soft bedding in his "room" (the crate), something he can snuggle into to feel cozy and secure. Old towels or blankets are good choices for a young pup, since he may (and probably will) have a toileting accident or two in the crate or decide to chew on the bedding material. Once he is fully trained and out of the early chewing stage, you can replace the puppy bedding with a permanent crate pad if you prefer. Crate pads

Your local pet shop should have a wide variety of crates to show you. A medium-size crate is suitable for the puppy and full-grown Whippet.

one, so the choice is up to you. The wire crates offer better visibility for the pup as well as better ventilation. Many of the wire crates collapse for ease of transport. The fiberglass crates, similar to those used by the airlines for animal transport, are sturdier and more den-like. However, the fiberglass crates do not collapse and are less ventilated than a wire crate, which can be problematic in hot weather. Some of the newer crates are made of heavy plastic mesh; they are very lightweight and fold up into slim-line suit-

ESTABLISH A ROUTINE

Routine is very important to a puppy's learning environment. To facilitate house-training, use the same exit/entrance door for potty trips and always take the puppy to the same place in the yard. The same principle of consistency applies to all other aspects of puppy training.

and other dog beds run the gamut from inexpensive to high-end doggie-designer styles, but don't splurge on the good stuff until you are sure that your puppy is reliable and won't tear it up or make a mess on it.

PUPPY TOYS

Just as infants and older children require objects to stimulate their minds and bodies, puppies need toys to entertain their curious brains, wiggly paws and achy teeth. A fun array of safe doggie toys will help satisfy your puppy's chewing instincts and distract him from gnawing on the leg of your antique chair or your new leather sofa. Most puppy toys are cute and look as if they would be a lot of fun, but not all are

As puppies and adults, Whippets enjoy each other's company.

necessarily safe or good for your puppy, so use caution when you go puppy-toy shopping.

Although Whippets are not known to be voracious chewers, they still, like most dogs, enjoy a good chew. The best "chewcifiers" are nylon and hard rubber bones, which are safe to gnaw on and come in sizes appropriate for all age groups and breeds. Be especially careful of natural bones, which can splinter or develop dangerous sharp edges; pups can easily swallow or choke on those bone splinters. Veterinarians often tell of surgical nightmares involving bits of splintered bone, because in addition to the danger of choking, the sharp pieces can damage the intestinal tract.

TEETHING TIME

All puppies chew. It's normal canine behavior. Chewing just plain feels good to a puppy, especially during the three- to five-month teething period when the adult teeth are breaking through the gums. Rather than attempting to eliminate such a strong natural chewing instinct, you will be more successful if you redirect it and teach your puppy what he may or may not chew. Correct inappropriate chewing with a sharp "No!" and offer him a chew toy, praising him when he takes it. Don't become discouraged. Chewing usually decreases after the adult teeth have come in.

Similarly, rawhide chews, while a favorite of most dogs and puppies, can be equally danger-ous. Pieces of rawhide are easily swallowed after they get all gummy from chewing, and dogs have been known to choke on large pieces of ingested rawhide. Rawhide chews should be offered only when you can supervise the puppy.

Soft woolly toys are special puppy favorites. They come in a wide variety of cute shapes and sizes; some look like little stuffed animals. Puppies love to shake them up and toss them about, or simply carry them around. Be careful of fuzzy toys that have button eyes or noses that your pup could chew off and swallow,

and make sure that he does not disembowel a squeaky toy to remove the squeaker! "De-squeaking" a toy is as instinctive to a Whippet as catching a runaway hare. Braided rope toys are similar in that they are fun to chew and toss around, but they shred easily and the strings are easy to swallow. The strings are not digestible and, if the puppy doesn't pass them in his stool, he could end up at the vet's office. As with rawhides, your puppy should be closely monitored with rope toys.

If you believe that your pup has ingested one of these forbid-den objects, check his stools for the next couple of days to see if he passes them when he defecates. At the same time, also watch for signs of intestinal distress. A call to your veterinarian might be in order to get his advice and be on the safe side.

An all-time favorite toy for puppies (young and old!) is the empty gallon milk jug. Hard plastic juice containers—46 ounces or more—are also excellent. Such containers make lots of noise when they are batted about, and puppies go crazy with delight as they play with them. However, they don't often last very long, so be sure to remove and replace them when they get chewed up.

A word of caution about homemade toys: be careful with your choices of non-traditional play objects. Never use old shoes or socks, since a puppy cannot distinguish between the old ones on which he's allowed to chew and the new ones in your closet that are strictly off-limits. That principle applies to anything that resembles something that you don't want your puppy to chew.

COLLARS

A lightweight nylon collar is the best choice for a very young pup. Quick-clip collars are easy to put on and remove, and they can be adjusted as the puppy grows. Introduce him to his collar as soon as he comes home to get him accustomed to wearing it. He'll get used to it quickly and won't mind a bit. Make sure that it is

TOYS 'R SAFE

The vast array of tantalizing puppy is staggering. Stroll through any pet shop or pet-supply outlet and you will see that the choices can be overwhelming. However, not all dog toys are safe or sensible. Most very young puppies enjoy soft woolly toys that they can snuggle with and carry around. (You know they have outgrown them when they shred them up!) Avoid toys that have buttons, tabs or other enhancements that can be chewed off and swallowed. Soft toys that squeak are fun, but make sure your puppy does not disembowel the toy and remove (and swallow) the squeaker. Toys that rattle or make noise can excite a puppy, but they present the same danger as the squeaky kind and so require supervision. Hard rubber toys that bounce can also entertain a pup, but make sure that the toy is too big for your pup to swallow.

COLLARING OUR CANINES

The standard flat collar with a buckle or a snap, in leather, nylon or cotton, is widely regarded as the everyday all-purpose collar. If the collar fits correctly, you should be able to fit two fingers between the collar and the dog's neck.

Leather Buckle Collars

Limited-Slip Collar

The martingale, Greyhound or limited-slip collar is preferred by many dog owners and trainers, especially for use with sighthounds, whose slender necks and heads make it easy for them to back out of a traditional buckle collar. It is fixed with an extra loop that tightens when pressure is applied to the leash. The martingale collar gets tighter but does not "choke" the dog. The limited-slip collar should only be used for walking and training, not for free play or interaction with another dog. These types of collar should never be left on the dog, as the extra loop can lead to accidents.

Choke collars, usually made of stainless steel, are made for training purposes, though are not recommended for small dogs, heavily coated breeds or fine-skinned breeds like the Whippet. The chains can injure small dogs or can damage long coats or thin skins. Thin nylon choke leads are commonly used on show dogs while in the ring, though they are not practical for everyday use.

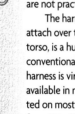

Snap Bolt Choke Collar

The harness, with two or three straps that attach over the dog's shoulders and around his torso, is a humane and safe alternative to the conventional collar. By and large, a well-made harness is virtually escape-proof. Harnesses are available in nylon and mesh and can be outfitted on most dogs, with chest girths ranging from 10 to 30 inches.

Harness

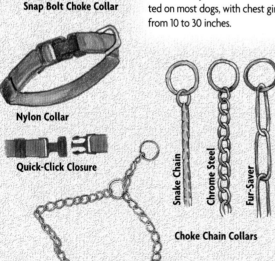

Nylon Collar

Quick-Click Closure

Choke Chain Collars

Snake Chain

Chrome Steel

Fur-Saver

A head collar, composed of a nylon strap that goes around the dog's muzzle and a second strap that wraps around his neck, offers the owner better control over his dog. This device is recommended for problem-solving with dogs (including jumping up, pulling and aggressive behaviors), but must be used with care.

A training halter, including a flat collar and two straps, made of nylon and webbing, is designed for walking. There are several on the market; some are more difficult to put on the dog than others. The halter harness, with two small slip rings at each end, is recommended for ease of use.

snug enough that it won't slip off, yet loose enough to be comfortable for the pup. You should be able to slip two fingers between the collar and his neck. Check the collar often, as puppies grow in spurts, and his collar can become too tight almost overnight. Martingale collars are recommended for training and walking sighthound breeds.

LEASHES

A 6-foot nylon lead is an excellent choice for a young puppy. It is lightweight and not as tempting to chew as a leather lead. You can switch to a 6-foot leather lead after your pup has grown and is used to walking politely on a lead. For initial puppy walks and house-training purposes, you should invest in a shorter lead so that you have more control over the puppy. At first, you don't want him wandering too far away from you, and when taking him out for toileting you will want to keep him in the specific area chosen for his potty spot.

Once the puppy is heel-trained with a traditional leash, you can consider purchasing a retractable lead. This type of lead is excellent for walking adult dogs that are already leash-wise. The retractable lead allows the dog to roam farther away from you and explore a wider area when out walking, and also retracts when you need to keep him close to you.

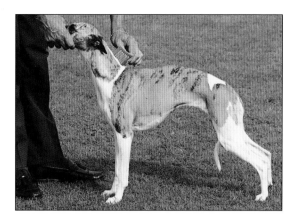

HOME SAFETY FOR YOUR PUPPY

The importance of puppy-proofing cannot be overstated. In addition to making your house comfortable for your Whippet's arrival, you also must make sure that your house is safe for your puppy before you bring him home. There are countless hazards in the owner's personal living environment that a pup can sniff, chew, swallow or destroy. Many are obvious; others are not. Do a thorough advance house check to remove or rearrange those things that could hurt your puppy, keeping any potentially dangerous items out of areas to which he will have access.

Electrical cords are especially dangerous, since puppies view them as irresistible chew toys. Unplug and remove all exposed cords or fasten them beneath the baseboards where the puppy cannot reach them. Veterinarians and firefighters can tell you

The Whippet does not require complicated grooming, but you will need to obtain some basic coat care tools.

Leash Life

Dogs love leashes! Believe it or not, most dogs dance for joy every time their owners pick up their leashes. The leash means that the dog is going for a walk—and there are few things more exciting than that! Here are some of the kinds of leashes that are commercially available.

Nylon Leash

Leather Leash

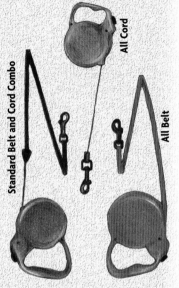

Standard Belt and Cord Combo

All Cord

All Belt

Retractable Leashes

Traditional Leash: Made of cotton, nylon or leather, these leashes are usually about 6 feet in length. A quality-made leather leash is softer on the hands than a nylon one. Durable woven cotton is a popular option. Lengths can vary up to about 48 feet, designed for different uses.

Chain Leash: Usually a metal chain leash with a plastic handle. This is not the best choice for most breeds, as it is heavier than other leashes and difficult to manage.

Retractable Leash: A long nylon cord is housed in a plastic device for extending and retracting. This type of leash is ideal for taking trained dogs for long walks in open areas, although it is not recommended for large, powerful breeds. Different lengths and sizes are available, so check that you purchase one appropriate for your dog's weight.

Elastic Leash: A nylon leash with an elastic extension. This is useful for well-trained dogs, especially in conjunction with a head halter. Avoid leashes that are completely elastic, as

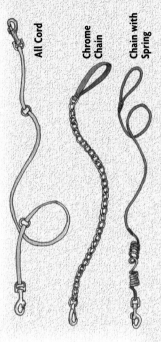

All Cord

Chrome Chain

Chain with Spring

they afford minimal control to the handler.

Adjustable Leash: This has two snaps, one on each end, and several metal rings. It is handy if you need to tether your dog temporarily, but is never to be used with a choke collar.

Tab Leash: A short leash (4 to 6 inches long) that attaches to your dog's collar. This device serves like a handle, in case you have to grab your dog while he's exercising off lead. It's ideal for "half-trained" dogs or dogs that listen only half the time.

Slip Leash: Essentially a leash with a collar built in, similar to what a dog-show handler uses to show a dog. This British-style collar has a ring on the end so that you can form a slip collar. Useful if you have to catch your own runaway dog or a stray.

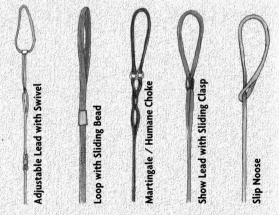

Adjustable Lead with Swivel

Loop with Sliding Bead

Martingale / Humane Choke

Show Lead with Sliding Clasp

Slip Noose

A Variety of Collar-and-Leash-in-One Products

to reach more and more as he grows taller.

Once your house has cleared inspection, check your yard. A sturdy fence, well embedded into the ground, will give your dog a safe place to play and potty. Although Whippets are not known to be climbers or fence jumpers, they are still athletic dogs, so a 5- to 6-foot-high fence will be necessary to contain an agile youngster or adult. Check the fence periodically for necessary repairs. If there is a weak link or space to squeeze through, you can be sure a determined Whippet will discover it.

The garage and shed can be hazardous places for a pup, as things like fertilizers, chemicals

horror stories about electrical burns and house fires that resulted from puppy-chewed electrical cords. Consider this a most serious precaution for your puppy and the rest of your family.

Scout your home for tiny objects that might be seen at a pup's eye level. Keep medication bottles and cleaning supplies well out of reach, and do the same with waste baskets and other trash containers. It goes without saying that you should not use rodent poison or other toxic chemicals in any puppy area and that you must keep such containers safely locked up. You will be amazed at how many places a curious puppy can discover, and he will be able

A wire pen, called an ex-pen, provides your dog with a larger area of safe confinement when outdoors in an unfenced area or when traveling.

A seven-week-old Whippet puppy finds it hard to resist chewing on forbidden things, like shoes and laces!

and tools are usually kept there. It's best to keep these areas off limits to the pup. Antifreeze is especially dangerous to dogs, as they find the taste appealing and it takes only a few licks from the driveway to kill a dog, puppy or adult, small breed or large.

VISITING THE VETERINARIAN

A good veterinarian is your Whippet puppy's best health-insurance policy. If you do not already have a vet, ask friends and experienced dog people in your area for recommendations so that you can select a vet before you bring your Whippet puppy home. Also arrange for

Puppyhood is such an exciting time. The Whippet puppy certainly endures awkward stages in which his ears develop, his limbs grow like vines and his coordination is not synchronized. Not to worry, time will sort everything out.

your puppy's first veterinary examination beforehand, since many vets do not have appointments available immediately and your puppy should visit the vet within a day or so of coming home.

It's important to make sure that your puppy's first visit to the vet is a pleasant and positive one. The vet should take great care to befriend the pup and handle him gently to make their first meeting a positive experience. The vet will give the pup a thorough physical examination and set up a schedule for vaccinations and other necessary wellness visits. Be sure to show your vet any health and inoculation records, which you

"Who, me?" An innocent-looking puppy, yet not too good at hiding the evidence!

should have received from your breeder. Your vet is a great source of canine health information, so be sure to ask questions and take notes. Creating a health journal for your puppy will make a handy reference for his wellness and any future health problems that may arise.

MEETING THE FAMILY

Your Whippet's homecoming is an exciting time for all members of the family, and it's only natural that everyone will be eager to meet him, pet him and play with

ASK THE VET

Help your vet help you to become a well-informed dog owner. Don't be shy about becoming involved in your puppy's veterinary care by asking questions and gaining as much knowledge as you can. For starters, ask what shots your puppy is getting and what diseases they prevent, and discuss with your vet the safest way to vaccinate. Find out what is involved in your dog's annual wellness visits. If you plan to spay or neuter, discuss the best age at which to have this done. Start out on the right "paw" with your puppy's vet and develop good communication with him, as he will care for your dog's health throughout the dog's entire life.

Puppies are among the most curious creatures in existence. Keep a watchful eye out whenever your Whippet is outside in the yard.

THE GRASS IS ALWAYS GREENER

Just as dog urine is no tonic for growing grass, lawn chemicals are extremely dangerous to your dog. Fertilizers, pesticides and herbicides pose real threats to canines and humans alike. Dogs should be kept off treated grounds for at least 24 hours following treatment. Consider some organic options for your lawn care, such as using a homemade compost or a natural fertilizer instead of a commercial chemical. Some dog-conscious lawnkeepers avoid fertilizers entirely, keeping up their lawns by watering, aerating, mowing and seeding frequently.

As always, dogs complicate the equation. Canines love grass. They roll in it, eat it and love to bury their noses in it—and then do their business in it! Grass can mean hours of feel-good, smell-good fun! In addition to the dangers of lawn-care chemicals, there's also the threat of burs, thorns and pebbles in the grass, not to mention the very common grass allergy. Many dogs develop an incurably itchy skin condition from grass, especially in the late summer when the world is in full bloom.

him. However, for the puppy's sake, it's best to make these initial family meetings as uneventful as possible so that the pup is not overwhelmed with too much too soon. Remember, he has just left his dam and his littermates and is away from the breeder's home for the first time. Despite his fuzzy wagging tail, he is still apprehensive and wondering where he is and who all these strange humans are. It's best to let him explore on his own and meet the family members as he feels comfortable. Let him investigate all the new smells, sights and sounds at his own pace. Children should be especially careful to not get overly excited, use loud voices or hug the pup too tightly. Be calm, gentle and affectionate, and be ready to comfort him if he appears frightened or uneasy.

Be sure to show your puppy his new crate during this first day home. Toss a treat or two inside the crate; if he associates the crate with food, he will associate the crate with good things. If he is comfortable with the crate, you can offer him his first meal inside it. Leave the door ajar so he can wander in and out as he chooses.

FIRST NIGHT IN HIS NEW HOME

So much has happened in your Whippet puppy's first day away from the breeder. He's had his first car ride to his new home. He's

TOXIC PLANTS

Plants are natural puppy magnets, but many can be harmful, even fatal, if ingested by a puppy or adult dog. Scout your yard and home interior and remove any plants, bushes or flowers that could be even mildly dangerous. It could save your puppy's life. You can obtain a complete list of toxic plants from your veterinarian, at the public library or by looking online.

met his new human family and perhaps the other family pets. He has explored his new house and yard, at least those places where

Since a Whippet can easily outrun his owner, keeping him in a securely enclosed area is the only way to ensure his safety when he's off lead.

A sighthound is a thing of beauty, with elegant lines and a gentle yet alert expression.

New owners are replacing a mother's love. Most Whippet dams are dependable, responsible parents who bond closely with their pups.

mates. Surely that's enough to tire out an eight-week-old Whippet pup...or so you hope!

It's bedtime. During the day, the pup investigated his crate, which is his new den and sleeping space, so it is not entirely strange to him. Line the crate with a soft towel or blanket that he can snuggle into and gently place him into the crate for the night. Some breeders send home a piece of bedding from where the pup slept with his littermates, and those familiar scents are a great comfort for the puppy on his first night without his siblings.

he is to be allowed during his first weeks at home. He may have visited his new veterinarian. He has eaten his first meal or two away from his dam and litter-

He will probably whine or cry. The puppy is objecting to the confinement and the fact that he is alone for the first time. This can be a stressful time for you as well as for the pup. It's important that you remain strong and don't let the puppy out of his crate to comfort him. He will fall asleep eventually. If you release him, the puppy will learn that crying means "out" and will continue that habit. You are laying the groundwork for future habits. Some breeders find that soft music can soothe a crying pup and help him get to sleep.

SOCIALIZING YOUR PUPPY

The first 20 weeks of your Whippet puppy's life are the most important of his entire lifetime. A properly socialized puppy will grow up to be a confident and stable adult who will be a pleasure to live with and a welcome addition to the neighborhood. The importance of socialization cannot be overemphasized. Research on canine behavior has proven that puppies who are not exposed to new sights, sounds, people and animals during their first 20 weeks of life will grow up to be timid and fearful, even aggressive, and unable to flourish outside of their home environment.

Socializing your puppy is not difficult and, in fact, will be a fun time for you both. Lead training goes hand in hand with socializa-

tion, so your puppy will be learning how to walk on a lead at the same time that he's meeting the neighborhood. Because the Whippet is such a terrific breed, your puppy will enjoy being "the new kid on the block." Take him for short walks, to the park and to other dog-friendly places where

A Whippet whose training begins early in life grows into an obedient adult.

BE CONSISTENT

Consistency is a key element, in fact is absolutely necessary, to a puppy's learning environment. A behavior (such as chewing, jumping up or climbing onto the furniture) cannot be forbidden one day and then allowed the next. That will only confuse the pup, and he will not understand what he is supposed to do. Just one or two episodes of allowing an undesirable behavior to "slide" will imprint that behavior on a puppy's brain and make that behavior more difficult to erase or change.

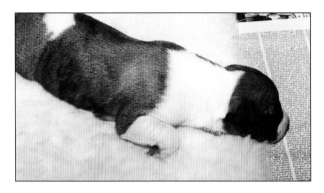

The whelping box serves as living room, dining room, bedroom and bathroom for very young pups. Breeders provide absorbent materials for the pups and must keep the area clean, changing the lining as needed throughout each day.

he will encounter new people, especially children. Puppies automatically recognize children as "little people" and are drawn to play with them. Just make sure that you supervise these meetings and that the children do not get too rough or encourage him to play too hard. Likewise, an overzealous pup can often nip too hard, frightening the child and in turn making the puppy overly excited. A bad experience in puppyhood can impact a dog for life, so a pup that has a negative experience with a child may grow up to be shy or even aggressive around children.

Take your puppy along on your daily errands. Puppies are natural "people magnets," and most people who see your pup will want to pet him. All of these encounters will help to mold him into a confident adult dog. Likewise, you will soon feel like a confident, responsible dog owner, rightly proud of your handsome Whippet.

Be especially careful of your puppy's encounters and experiences during the eight-to-ten-week-old period, which is also called the "fear period." This is a serious imprinting period, and all contact during this time should be gentle and positive. A frightening or negative event could leave a permanent impression that could affect his future behavior if a similar situation arises.

Also make sure that your puppy has received his first and second rounds of vaccinations before you expose him to other dogs or bring him to places that other dogs may frequent. Avoid dog parks and other strange-dog areas until your vet assures you that your puppy is fully immunized and resistant to the diseases that can be passed between canines. Discuss socialization with your breeder, as some breeders recommend socializing the puppy even before he has received all of his inoculations, depending on how outgoing the puppy may be.

LEADER OF THE PUPPY'S PACK
Like other canines, your puppy needs an authority figure, someone he can look up to and regard as the leader of his "pack." His first pack leader was his dam, who taught him to be polite and not to chew too hard on her ears or nip at her muzzle. He learned those same lessons from his litter-

mates. If he played too rough, they cried in pain and stopped the game, which sent an important message to the rowdy puppy.

As puppies play together, they are also struggling to determine who will be the boss. Being pack animals, dogs need someone to be in charge. If a litter of puppies remained together beyond puppyhood, one of the pups would emerge as the strongest one, the one who calls the shots.

Once your puppy leaves the pack, he will look intuitively for a new leader. If he does not recognize you as that leader, he will try to assume that position for himself. Of course, it is hard to imagine your adorable Whippet puppy trying to be in charge when he is so small and seemingly helpless. You must remember that these are natural canine instincts. Do not cave in and allow your pup to get the upper "paw"!

Just as socialization is so important during these first 20 weeks, so too is your puppy's early education. He was born without any bad habits. He does not know what is good or bad behavior. If he does things like nipping and digging, it's because he is having fun and doesn't know that humans consider these things as "bad." It's your job to teach him proper puppy manners, and this is the best time to accomplish that...before he has developed bad habits, since it is much more diffi-

cult to "unlearn" or correct unacceptable learned behavior than to teach good behavior from the start.

Make sure that all members of the family understand the importance of being consistent when training the new puppy. If you tell the puppy to stay off the sofa and your daughter allows him to cuddle on the couch to watch her favorite television show, your pup will be confused about what he is and is not allowed to do. Have a

Is it any surprise that the striking Whippet creates a scene in show rings around the globe?

HAPPY PUPPIES COME RUNNING

Never call your puppy (or adult dog) to come to you and then scold him or discipline him when he gets there. He will make a natural association between coming to you and being scolded, and he will think he was a bad dog for coming to you. He will then be reluctant to come whenever he is called. Always praise your puppy every time he comes to you.

family conference before your pup comes home so that everyone understands the basic principles of puppy training and the rules you have set forth for the pup, and agrees to follow them.

PREVENTING AND SOLVING PUPPY PROBLEMS

The old saying that "an ounce of prevention is worth a pound of cure" is especially true when it comes to puppies. It is much easier to prevent inappropriate

Puppies are very oral, often playing mouth games with their littermates. Puppies are always jostling for position in the pack.

behavior than it is to change it. It's also easier and less stressful for the pup, since it will keep discipline to a minimum and create a more positive learning environment for him. That, in turn, will also be easier on you!

Here are a few commonsense tips to keep your belongings safe and your puppy out of trouble:

- Keep your closet doors closed and your shoes, socks and other apparel off the floor so your puppy can't get at them.
- Keep a secure lid on the trash container or put the trash where your puppy can't dig into it. He can't damage what he can't reach!
- Supervise your puppy at all times to make sure he is not getting into mischief. If he starts to chew the corner of the rug, you can distract him instantly by tossing a toy for him to fetch. You also will be able to whisk him outside when you notice that he is about to piddle on the carpet. If you can't see your puppy, you can't teach him or correct his behavior.

CHEWING AND NIPPING

Nipping at fingers and toes is normal puppy behavior. Chewing is also the way that puppies investigate their surroundings. However, you will have to teach your puppy that chewing on anything other than his toys is not acceptable. That won't happen

REPEAT YOURSELF
Puppies learn best through repetition. Use the same verbal cues and commands when teaching your puppy new behaviors or correcting for misbehaviors. Be consistent, but not monotonous. Puppies get bored just like puppy owners.

overnight and at times puppy teeth will test your patience. However, if you allow nipping and chewing to continue, just think about the damage that a mature Whippet can do with a full set of adult teeth.

Whenever your puppy nips your hand or fingers, cry out "Ouch!" in a loud voice, which should startle your puppy and stop him from nipping, even if only for a moment. Immediately distract him by offering a small treat or an appropriate toy for him to chew instead (which means having chew toys and puppy treats handy at all times). Praise him when he takes the toy and tell him what a good fellow he is. Praise is just as or even more important in puppy training as discipline and correction.

Puppies also tend to nip at children more often than adults, since they perceive little ones to be more vulnerable and more similar to their littermates. Teach your children appropriate responses to nipping behavior. If they are unable to handle it themselves, you may have to intervene. Puppy nips can be quite painful and a child's frightened reaction will only encourage a puppy to nip harder, which is a natural canine response. As with all other puppy situations, interaction between your Whippet puppy and children should be supervised.

Chewing on objects, not just family members' fingers and ankles, is also normal canine behavior that can be especially tedious (for the owner, not the pup) during the teething period when the puppy's adult teeth are coming in. At this stage, chewing just plain feels good. Furniture legs and cabinet corners are common puppy favorites. Shoes and other personal items also taste pretty good to a pup.

The best solution is, once again, prevention. If you value something, keep it tucked away and out of reach. You can't hide your dining-room table in a closet, but you can try to deflect the chewing by applying a bitter product made for the purpose of deterring dogs from chewing. Available in a spray or cream, this substance is vile-tasting, although safe for dogs, and most puppies will avoid the forbidden object after one tiny taste. You also can apply the product to the pup's leash if the puppy tries to chew on it during leash-training sessions.

Keep a ready supply of safe chews handy to offer your Whippet as a distraction when he starts to chew on something that's a "no-no." Remember, at this tender age, he does not yet know what is permitted or forbidden, so you have to be "on call" every minute he's awake and on the prowl.

You may lose a treasure or two during puppy's growing-up period, and the furniture could sustain a nasty nick or two. These can be trying times, so be prepared for those inevitable accidents and comfort yourself in knowing that this too shall pass.

WATCH THE WATER
To help your puppy sleep through the night without having to relieve himself, remove his water bowl after 7 p.m. Offer him a couple of ice cubes during the evening to quench his thirst. Never leave water in a puppy's crate, as this is inviting puddles of mishaps.

PUPPY WHINING

Puppies often cry and whine, just as infants and little children do. It's their way of telling us that they are lonely or in need of attention. Your puppy will miss his littermates and will feel insecure when he is left alone. You may be out of the house or just in another room, but he will still feel alone. During these times, the puppy's crate should be his personal comfort station, a place all his own where he can feel safe and secure. Once he learns that being alone is okay and not something to be feared, he will settle down without crying or objecting. You might want to leave a radio on while he is crated, as the sound of human voices can be soothing and will give the impression that people are around.

Give your puppy a favorite cuddly toy or chew toy to entertain him whenever he is crated. You will both be happier: the puppy because he is safe in his den and you because he is quiet, safe and not getting into puppy escapades that can wreak havoc in your house or cause him danger.

To make sure that your puppy will always view his crate as a safe and cozy place, never, ever, use the crate as punishment. That's the best way to turn the crate into a negative place that the pup will want to avoid. Sure, you can use the crate for your own peace of mind if your puppy is getting into

trouble and needs some "time out." Just don't let him know that! Never scold the pup and immediately place him into the crate. Count to ten, give him a couple of hugs and maybe a treat, then scoot him into his crate.

It's also important not to make a big fuss when he is released from the crate. That will make getting out of the crate more appealing than being in the crate, which is just the opposite of what you are trying to achieve.

Whippets and their human "siblings" form a strong bond of friendship.

Adding a Whippet to your household means adding a new family member who will need your care each and every day. When your Whippet pup first comes home, you will start a routine with him so that, as he grows up, your dog will have a daily schedule just as you do. The aspects of your dog's daily care will likewise become regular parts of your day, so you'll both have a new schedule. Dogs learn by consistency and thrive on routine: regular times for meals, exercise, grooming and potty trips are just as important for your dog as they are to you! Your dog's

schedule will depend much on your family's daily routine, but remember that you now have a new member of the family who is part of your day every day.

FEEDING

Feeding your dog the best diet is based on various factors, including age, activity level, overall condition and size. When you visit the breeder, he will share with you his advice about the proper diet for your dog based on his experience with the breed and the foods with which he has had success. Likewise, your vet will be a helpful source of advice throughout the dog's life and will aid you in planning a diet for optimal health.

FEEDING THE PUPPY

Of course, your pup's very first food will be his dam's milk. There may be special situations in which pups fail to nurse, necessitating that the breeder hand-feed them with a formula, but for the most part pups spend the first weeks of life nursing from their dam. The breeder weans the pups

FREE FEEDING

Many owners opt to feed their dogs by serving dry kibble in a feeder, that is available to the dog all day. Arguably, this is the most convenient method of feeding an adult dog, but it is best to stick to scheduled feedings so you can allow him adequate rest between mealtimes and exercise sessions (and vice versa). Further, scheduled feedings are better for house-training purposes and for gauging your dog's appetite and recognizing any changes.

by gradually introducing solid foods and decreasing the milk meals. Pups may even start themselves off on the weaning process, albeit inadvertently, if they snatch bites from their mom's food bowl.

By the time the pups are ready for new homes, they are fully weaned and eating a good puppy food. As a new owner, you may be thinking, "Great! The breeder has taken care of the hard part." Not so fast.

A puppy's first year of life is the time when all or most of his growth and development takes place. This is a delicate time, and diet plays a huge role in proper skeletal and muscular formation. Improper diet and exercise habits can lead to damaging problems that will compromise the dog's health and movement for his entire life. That being said, new owners should not worry needlessly. With the myriad types of food formulated specifically for growing pups of different-sized breeds, dog-food manufacturers have taken much of the guesswork out of feeding your puppy well. Since growth-food formulas are designed to provide the nutrition that a growing puppy needs, it is unnecessary and, in fact, can prove harmful to add supplements to the diet. Research has shown that too much of certain vitamin supplements and minerals predispose a dog to skeletal problems. It's by no means a case of "if a

little is good, a lot is better." At every stage of your dog's life, too much or too little in the way of nutrients can be harmful, which is why a manufactured complete food is the easiest way to know that your dog is getting what he needs.

Because of a young pup's small body and accordingly small digestive system, his daily portion will be divided up into small meals throughout the day. This can mean starting off with three or more meals a day and decreasing the number of meals as the pup matures. It is generally thought that dividing the day's food into two meals on a morning/evening schedule is healthier for the dog's digestion.

Regarding the feeding schedule, feeding the pup at the same times and in the same place each day is important for both house-

Puppies instinctively suckle from their mother's teats almost immediately following birth. If they fail to do so, the breeder must hand-feed them until they are old enough to be weaned. There is no better food for the young puppy than mother's milk.

training purposes and establishing the dog's everyday routine. As for the amount to feed, growing puppies generally need proportionately more food per body weight than their adult counterparts, but a pup should never be allowed to

Many dogs enjoy the taste of canned foods, so a bit of canned food added to the dog's dry-food portions or as a special treat will be welcomed.

gain excess weight. Dogs of all ages should be kept in proper body condition, but extra weight can strain a pup's developing frame, causing skeletal problems.

Watch your pup's weight as he grows and, if the recommended amounts seem to be too much or

too little for your pup, consult the vet about appropriate dietary changes. Keep in mind that treats, although small, can quickly add up throughout the day, contributing unnecessary calories. Treats are fine when used prudently; opt for dog treats specially formulated to be healthy or for nutritious snacks like small pieces of cheese or cooked chicken.

FEEDING THE ADULT DOG

For the adult (meaning physically mature) dog, feeding properly is about maintenance, not growth. Again, correct weight is a concern. Your dog should appear fit and should have an evident "waist." His ribs should not be protruding (a sign of being underweight), but they should be covered by only a slight layer of fat. Under normal circumstances, an adult dog can be maintained fairly easily with a high-quality nutritionally complete adult-formula food.

Factor treats into your dog's overall daily caloric intake, and avoid offering table scraps. Some "people foods," like chocolate, onions, grapes, raisins and nuts are toxic to dogs. Plus, too many tidbits encourages begging and overeating. Overweight dogs are more prone to health problems. Research has even shown that obesity takes years off a dog's life. With that in mind, resist the urge to overfeed and over-treat. Don't make unnecessary additions to your dog's diet, whether with tidbits or with extra vitamins and minerals.

The amount of food needed for proper maintenance will vary depending on the individual dog's activity level, but you will be able to tell whether the daily portions are keeping him in good shape. With the wide variety of good complete foods available, choosing what to feed is largely a matter of personal preference. Just as with the puppy, the adult dog should have consistency in his mealtimes and feeding place. In addition to a consistent routine, regular mealtimes also allow the owner to see how much his dog is eating. If the dog seems never to be satisfied or, likewise, becomes uninterested in his food, the owner will know right away that something is wrong and can consult the vet.

DIETS FOR THE AGING DOG

A good rule of thumb is that once a dog has reached 75% of his expected lifespan, he has reached "senior citizen" or geriatric status. Your Whippet will be considered a senior when he is about 10 years of age; based on his size, he has a projected lifespan of about 14 years.

What does aging have to do with your dog's diet? No, he won't get a discount at the local diner's early-bird special. Yes, he will

> **HOLD THE ONIONS**
> Sliced, chopped or grated; dehydrated, boiled, fried or raw; pearl, Spanish, white or red: onions can be deadly to your dog. The toxic effects of onions in dogs are cumulative for up to 30 days. A serious form of anemia, called Heinz body anemia, affects the red blood cells of dogs that have eaten onions. For safety (and better breath), dogs should avoid chives and scallions as well.

require some dietary changes to accommodate the changes that come along with increased age. One change is that the older dog's dietary needs become more similar to that of a puppy. Specifically, dogs can metabolize more protein as youngsters and seniors than in the adult-maintenance stage. Discuss with your vet whether you need to switch to a higher-protein or senior-formulated food or whether your current adult-dog

After several years of puppy exuberance, Whippets tend to become more restful and calm, making fine companions for young and old alike. This young lady has a lovely rapport with her equally lovely Whippet.

TYPES OF FOOD AND READING THE LABEL

When selecting the type of food to feed your dog, it is important to check out the label for ingredients. Many dry-food products have soybean, corn or rice as the main ingredient. The main ingredient will be listed first on the label, with the rest of the ingredients following in descending order according to their proportion in the food. While these types of dry food are fine, you should look into dry foods based on meat or fish. These are better-quality foods and thus higher priced. However, they may be just as economical in the long run, because studies have shown that it takes less of the higher-quality foods to maintain a dog.

Comparing the various types of food—dry, canned and semi-moist—dry foods contain the least amount of water and canned foods the most. Proportionately, dry foods are the most calorie- and nutrient-dense, which means that you need more of a canned food product to supply the same amount of nutrition. In households with breeds of different sizes, the canned/dry/semi-moist question can be of special importance. Larger breeds obviously eat more than smaller ones and thus in general do better on dry foods, but smaller breeds do fine on canned foods and require "small bite" formulations to protect their small mouths and teeth if fed only

There are proponents of fresh- and raw-food diets, but an owner must be thoroughly educated in this type of diet before attempting it with his dog. Pears, for example, are far from standard Whippet fare.

food contains sufficient nutrition for the senior.

Watching the dog's weight remains essential, even more so in the senior stage. Older dogs are already more vulnerable to illness, and obesity only contributes to their susceptibility to problems. As the older dog becomes less active and thus exercises less, his regular portions may cause him to gain weight. At this point, you may consider decreasing his daily food intake or switching to a reduced-calorie food. As with other changes, you should consult your vet for advice.

dry foods. So if you have different-sized breeds in your household, consider both your own preferences and what your dogs like to eat. As a rule of thumb, though, think canned for the little guys and dry or semi-moist for everyone else. You may find success mixing the food types as well. Water is important for all dogs, but even more so for those fed dry foods, as there is no high water content in their food.

There are strict controls that regulate the nutritional content of dog food, and a food has to meet the minimum requirements in order to be considered "complete and balanced." It is important that you choose such a food for your dog, so check the label to be sure that your chosen food meets the requirements. If not, look for a food that clearly states on the label that it is formulated to be complete and balanced for your dog's particular stage of life.

Recommendations for amounts to feed will also be indicated on the label. You should also ask your vet about proper food portions, and you will keep an eye on your dog's condition to see whether the recommended amounts are adequate. If he becomes over- or underweight, you will need to make adjustments; this also would be a good time to consult your vet.

The food label may also make feeding suggestions, such as

whether moistening a dry-food product is recommended. Beware, though, if water makes a dry food swell up, as this will introduce air into your dog's system, which is very unhealthy. Don't be overwhelmed by the many factors that

Produce a tasty morsel and watch a crowd gather!

go into feeding your dog. Manufacturers of complete and balanced foods make it easy, and once you find the right food and amounts for your Whippet, his daily feeding will be a matter of routine.

DON'T FORGET THE WATER!

For a dog, it's always time for a drink! Regardless of what type of food he eats, there's no doubt that he needs plenty of water. Fresh cold water, in a clean bowl, should be made available to your

Sporting pursuits like agility trials provide excellent outlets for Whippets to expend their energy. Whippets require more exercise than many other dogs and welcome new challenges.

Water is the best drink for dogs. Some owners are tempted to give milk from time to time or to moisten dry food with milk, but dogs do not have the enzymes necessary to digest the lactose in milk, which is much different from the milk that nursing puppies receive. Therefore stick with clean fresh water to quench your dog's thirst, and always have it readily available to him.

EXERCISE

We all know the importance of exercise for humans, so it should come as no surprise that it is essential for our canine friends as well. To retain muscle tone and vitality, a Whippet must have regular exercise.

dog at all times. There are special circumstances, such as during puppy housebreaking, when you will want to monitor your pup's water intake so that you will be able to predict when he will need to relieve himself, but water must be available to him nonetheless. Water is essential for hydration and proper body function just as it is in humans.

You will get to know how much your dog typically drinks in a day. Of course, in the heat or if exercising vigorously, he will be more thirsty and will drink more. However, if he begins to drink noticeably more water for no apparent reason, this could signal any of various problems, and you are advised to consult your vet.

Just as with anything else you do with your dog, you must set a routine for his exercise. If you plan it and get into the habit of actually doing it, it will become just another part of your day. Think of it as making daily exercise appointments with your dog, and stick to your schedule. Whippets are easy to walk, and most breeders advocate a combination of on-lead walking and free runs in safely enclosed areas. Whippets amuse each other and thus will get additional exercise by playing if they spend time together.

As a rule, dogs in normal health should have at least half an hour of activity each day. Dogs with health or orthopedic problems may have specific limitations, so their exercise plans are best devised with the help of a vet. For healthy dogs, there are many ways to fit 30 minutes of activity into your day. Depending on your schedule, you may plan a 15-minute walk or activity session in the morning and again in the evening, or do it all at once in a half-hour session each day. Aside from walking, which is good for you, too, other suggestions include retrieving games, jogging and disc-catching or other active games with his toys. If you have a safe body of water nearby and a dog that likes to swim, swimming is an excellent form of exercise for dogs, putting no stress on his frame.

On that note, some precautions should be taken with a puppy's exercise. During his first year, when he is growing and developing, your Whippet should not be subject to stressful activity that stresses his body. Short walks at a comfortable pace and play sessions in the yard are good for a growing pup, and his exercise can be increased as he grows up.

For overweight dogs, dietary changes and activity will help the goal of weight loss (sound familiar?). While they should of course be encouraged to be active, remember not to overdo it, as the excess weight is already putting strain on his vital organs and bones. As for highly active dogs,

DOGGIE SPF
Modern science has emphasized the importance of sunscreen for ourselves and taking precautions in the sun. Some of these principles apply to dogs, too. Dogs with heavy and/or dark-colored coats are more vulnerable to overheating (you wouldn't wear a black wool sweater in the summertime, would you?). Likewise, dogs with short coats of light colors, like your Whippet, can become sunburned and will benefit from a light coating of sunblock (at least SPF 35) on exposed areas such as the nose, ears and belly.

some of them never seem to tire! They will enjoy time spent with their owners doing all kinds of things together.

Regardless of your dog's condition and activity level, exercise offers benefits to all dogs and owners. Consider the fact that dogs who are kept active are more stimulated both physically and mentally, meaning that they are less likely to become bored and lapse into destructive behavior. Also consider the benefits of one-on-one time with your dog every day, continually strengthening the bond between the two of you. Furthermore, exercising together will improve health and longevity for both of you. You both need exercise, and now you and your dog have a workout partner and motivator!

GROOMING

BRUSHING

With their short coats, Whippets require minimal grooming compared with many other breeds. Nonetheless, you should follow a routine grooming pattern. Only if attention is paid to coat, skin and nails will they remain in tip-top condition so that your dog will not only look but also feel its best.

Short grooming sessions should be introduced from an early age. From the very beginning, a few minutes each day should be set aside, the duration building up slightly as the puppy matures. Your puppy should be taught to stand calmly and quietly for grooming and for massage, both of which your dog will learn to enjoy.

ROUTINE MAINTENANCE

Each owner has his own favorite way of grooming his dog, and hopefully other owners with whom you come into contact will freely pass on some of their tips. Incidentally, Whippets benefit from massage, for this helps to tone up the muscles. Using a grooming glove massages the dog as you groom and offers some benefits in that regard.

A special rubber pad or grooming glove should be used to take out any dead hair. Various slightly differing gloves are available, some with very fine, short bristles

Hound gloves are a favorite with many Whippet owners. Gloves make grooming quick and easy, efficiently removing dead hair and dust from the coat.

attached to one side of the glove. A chamois leather, velvet or even a piece of silk can be used for finishing off. A useful grooming glove has chamois leather on one side and velvet on the other, which I find a very good combination.

If a dog has dandruff problems, a small amount of non-oily coat dressing can be applied, but this should be done at least a day before a show so that no residue is left in the coat. Owners generally like to carefully tidy up stray hairs under the tail and, if necessary, down the buttocks.

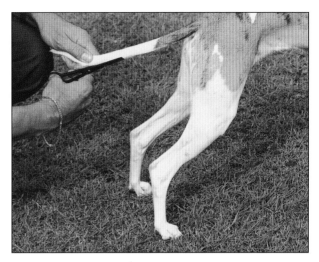

BATHING AND DRYING

How frequently you decide to bathe your Whippet will depend very much on personal preference and the lifestyle led by your hound. Many Whippets are bathed occasionally just to freshen them up, while some people prefer to bathe regularly before most shows, especially if their dogs are parti-colored or have white in their coats.

When bathing one of my own dogs, I like him to stand on a non-slip mat in the bath, then I wet the coat thoroughly using a shower spray attachment. It is imperative that the water temperature is first tested on your own hand. Use a good-quality shampoo designed especially for dogs. When it has been thoroughly rinsed out, you may apply a canine conditioner if you wish, and then rinse again

until the water runs clear. Many people like to use a baby shampoo on the head to avoid irritation to the eyes, and some like to plug the ears with cotton balls to avoid getting water inside them. Just take special care, and you shouldn't encounter problems. Towel-dry your dog while he's still in the bath and then help your Whippet carefully out of the tub. Undoubtedly your Whippet will want to shake—so be prepared!

If bathing during warm weather or in a heated home, drying this short-coated breed can be done more or less naturally. Never allow a dog to get cold after a bath; make sure the environment is pleasantly warm and never allow your hound outdoors in cold weather until the coat is completely dry.

It is always worth remembering that if you really feel your

Hairs on the Whippet's tail are often trimmed to give the tail a neater appearance.

dog's coat needs cleaning before a show but the weather is too cold, a dry shampoo can be used to freshen the coat. A dry bath can also be done for convenience between wet baths.

NAIL CLIPPING

Having his nails trimmed is not on many dogs' lists of favorite things to do. With this in mind, you will need to accustom your puppy to the procedure at a young age so that he will sit still (well, as still as he can) for his pedicures. Long nails can cause the dog's feet to spread, which is not good for him; likewise, long nails

can hurt if they unintentionally scratch, not good for you!

Some dogs' nails are worn down naturally by regular walking on hard surfaces, so the frequency with which you clip depends on your individual dog. Look at his nails from time to time and clip as needed; a good way to know when it's time for a trim is if you hear your dog clicking as he walks across the floor.

There are several types of nail clippers and even electric nail-grinding tools made for dogs; first we'll discuss using the clipper. To start, have your clipper ready and some doggie treats on hand. You want your pup to view his nail-clipping sessions in a positive light, and what better way to convince him than with food? You may want to enlist the help of an assistant to comfort the pup and offer treats as you concentrate on the clipping itself. The guillotine-type clipper is thought of by many as the easiest type to use; the nail tip is inserted into the opening, and blades on the top and bottom snip it off in one clip.

Start by grasping the pup's paw; a little pressure on the foot pad causes the nail to extend, making it easier to clip. Clip off a little at a time. If you can see the "quick," which is a blood vessel that runs through each nail, you will know how much to trim, as you do not want to cut into the quick. On that note, if you do cut

---

THE EARS KNOW

Examining your puppy's ears helps ensure good internal health. The ears are the eyes to the dog's innards! Begin handling your puppy's ears when he's still young so that he doesn't protest every time you lift a flap or touch his ears. Yeast and bacteria are two of the culprits that you can detect by examining the ear. You will notice a strong, often foul, odor, debris, redness or some kind of discharge. All of these point to health problems that can worsen over time. Additionally, you are on the lookout for wax accumulation, ear mites and other tiny bothersome parasites and their even tinier droppings. You may have to pluck hair with tweezers in order to have a better view into the dog's ears, but this is painless if done carefully.

the quick, which will cause bleeding, you can stem the flow of blood with a styptic pencil or other clotting agent. If you mistakenly nip the quick, do not panic or fuss, as this will cause the pup to be afraid. Simply reassure the pup, stop the bleeding and move on to the next nail. Don't be discouraged; you will become a professional canine pedicurist with practice.

You may or may not be able to see the quick, so it's best to just

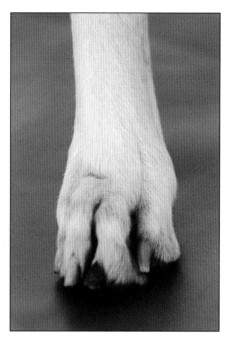

This is the front paw of a Whippet. A Whippet may have both light and dark nails.

clip off a small bit at a time. If you see a dark dot in the center of the nail, this is the quick and your cue to stop clipping. Tell the puppy he's a "good boy" and offer a piece of treat with each nail. You can also use nail-clipping time to examine the footpads, making sure that they are not dry and cracked and that nothing has become embedded in them.

SCOOTING HIS BOTTOM

Here's a doggy problem that many owners tend to neglect. If your dog is scooting his rear end around the carpet, he probably is experiencing anal-sac impaction or blockage. The anal sacs are the two grape-sized glands on either side of the dog's vent. The dog cannot empty these glands, which become filled with a foul-smelling material. The dog may attempt to lick the area to relieve the pressure. He may also rub his anus on your walls, furniture or floors.

Don't neglect your dog's rear end during grooming sessions. By squeezing both sides of the anus with a soft cloth, you can express some of the material in the sacs. If the material is pasty and thick, you likely will need the assistance of a veterinarian. Vets know how to express the glands and can show you how to do it correctly without hurting the dog or spraying yourself with the unpleasant liquid.

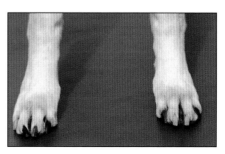

This is the back foot, showing well-trimmed nails.

The nail grinder, the other option, is many owners' first choice. Accustoming the puppy to the sound of the grinder and sensation of the buzz presents fewer challenges than the clipper, and there's no chance of cutting through the quick. Use the grinder on a low setting and always talk soothingly to your dog. He won't mind his salon visit, and he'll have nicely polished nails as well. The Whippet's nails are very important and must have a good finish. The grinder should accomplish this but, if using a clipper, the nails must be filed as well.

EYE CARE

During grooming sessions, pay extra attention to the condition of your dog's eyes. If the area around the eyes is soiled or if tear staining has occurred, there are various cleaning agents made especially for this purpose. Look at the dog's eyes to make sure no debris has entered; dogs with large eyes and those who spend time outdoors are especially prone to this.

The signs of an eye infection are obvious: mucus, redness, puffiness, scabs or other signs of irritation. If your dog's eyes become infected, the vet will likely prescribe an antibiotic ointment for treatment. If you notice signs of more serious problems, such as opacities in the eye, which usually indicate cataracts, consult the vet at once. Taking time to pay attention to your dog's eyes will alert you in the early stages of any problem so that you can get your dog treatment as soon as possible. You could save your dog's sight!

PRESERVING THOSE PEARLY WHITES

What do you treasure more than the smile of your beloved canine pal? Brushing your dog's teeth is just as important as brushing your own. Neglecting your dog's teeth can lead to tooth loss, periodontal disease and inflamed gums, not to mention bad breath. Can you find the time to brush your dog's teeth every day? If not, you should do so once a week at the very least, though every day is truly the ideal. Your vet should give your dog a thorough dental examination during his annual check-ups.

Pet shops sell terrific tooth-care devices, including specially designed toothbrushes, yummy toothpastes and finger-model brushes. You can use a human toothbrush with soft bristles, but never use human toothpastes, which can damage the dog's enamel. Baking soda is an alternative to doggy toothpastes, but your dog will be more receptive to canine toothpastes with the flavor of liver or hamburger. Make tooth care fun for your dog. Let him think that you're "horsing around" with his mouth. When brushing the dog's teeth, begin with the largest teeth (the canines) and proceed back toward the molars.

IDENTIFYING YOUR DOG

You love your Whippet and want to keep him safe. Of course you take every precaution to prevent his escaping from the yard or becoming lost or stolen. You have a sturdy high fence and you always keep your dog on-lead when out and about in public places. If your dog is not properly identified, however, you are overlooking a major aspect of his safety. We hope to never be in a situation where our dog is missing, but we should practice prevention in the unfortunate case that this happens; identification greatly increases the chances of your dog's being returned to you.

There are several ways to identify your dog. First, the traditional dog tag should be a staple in your dog's wardrobe, attached to his everyday collar. Tags can be made of sturdy plastic and various metals and should include your contact information so that a person who finds the dog can get in touch with you right away to arrange his return. Many people today enjoy the wide range of decorative tags available, so have fun and create a tag to match your dog's personality. Of course, it is important that the tag stays on the collar, so have a secure "O" ring attachment; you also can explore the type of tag that slides right onto the collar.

In addition to the ID tag, which every dog should wear even if identified by another method, two other forms of identification have become popular: microchipping and tattooing. In microchipping, a tiny scannable chip is painlessly inserted under the dog's skin. The number is registered to you so that, if your lost dog turns up at a clinic or shelter, the chip can be scanned to retrieve your contact information.

The advantage of the microchip is that it is a permanent form of ID, but there are some factors to consider. Several different companies make microchips, and not all are compatible with the others' scanning devices. It's best to find a company with a universal microchip that can be read by scanners made by other

CAR CAUTION

You may like to bring your canine companion along on the daily errands, but if you will be running in and out from place to place and can't bring him indoors with you, leave him at home. Your dog should never be left alone in the car, not even for a minute—never! A car can heat up very quickly in any kind of weather, and even a cracked-open window will not help. In fact, leaving the window cracked will be dangerous if the dog becomes uncomfortable and tries to escape. When in doubt, leave your dog home, where you know he will be safe.

The Whippet loves to be out and about in sunny weather, but provisions need to be made to protect him from the heat and sun.

companies as well. It won't do any good to have the dog chipped if the information cannot be retrieved. Also, not every humane society, shelter and clinic is equipped with a scanner, although more and more facilities are equipping themselves. In fact, many shelters microchip dogs that they adopt out to new homes.

Because the microchip is not visible to the eye, the dog must wear a tag that states that he is microchipped so that whoever picks him up will know to have him scanned. He of course also should have a tag with contact

Don't risk your Whippet's safety. A tattoo in an area where it is easily visible is insurance against dog theft. This photo has been retouched for clarity to show the tattoo on the dog's thigh.

YOUR PACK ANIMAL

If you are bringing your dog along with you on a vacation, here's a list of the things you want to pack for him:
- leashes (conventional and retractable)
- collar with ID tag
- dog food and bottled water
- grooming tools
- flea and tick sprays
- crate and crate pad
- pooper-scooper and plastic bags
- toys and treats
- towels and paper towels
- first-aid kit
- dog license and rabies certificate

another permanent method of ID for dogs. Most vets perform this service, and there are also clinics that perform dog tattooing. This is also an affordable procedure and one that will not cause much discomfort for the dog. It is best to put the tattoo in a visible area, such as the ear or inner thigh, to deter theft. It is sad to say that there are cases of dogs' being stolen and sold to research laboratories, but such laboratories will not accept tattooed dogs.

To ensure that the tattoo is effective in aiding your dog's return to you, the tattoo number must be registered with a national organization. That way, when someone finds a tattooed dog, a phone call to the registry will quickly match the dog with his owner.

information in case his chip cannot be read. Humane societies and veterinary clinics offer this service, which is usually very affordable.

Though less popular than microchipping, tattooing is

Select a boarding kennel that is clean, well-staffed with friendly dog people and spacious enough to provide each dog with ample room for exercise.

TRAINING YOUR
WHIPPET

With your attention to his training, your Whippet's behavior will befit his elegant, dignified appearance.

When you first bring the puppy home, he is eager to please you. This means that he accepts doing things your way. During the next couple of months, he will absorb the basis of everything he needs to know for the rest of his life. This early age is even referred to as the "sponge" stage. After that, for the next 18 months, it's

BASIC TRAINING PRINCIPLES: PUPPY VS. ADULT

There's a big difference between training an adult dog and training a young puppy. With a young puppy, everything is new. At eight to ten weeks of age, he will be experiencing many things, and he has nothing with which to compare these experiences. Up to this point, he has been with his dam and littermates, not one-on-one with people except in his interactions with his breeder and visitors to the litter.

THE RIGHT START

The best advice for a potential dog owner is to start with the very best puppy that money can buy. Don't shop around for a bargain in the newspaper. You're buying a companion, not a used car or a second-hand appliance. The purchase price of the dog represents a very significant part of the investment, but this is indeed a very small sum compared to the expenses of maintaining the dog in good health. If you purchase a well-bred, healthy and sound puppy, you will be starting right. An unhealthy puppy can cost you thousands of dollars in unnecessary veterinary expenses and, possibly, a fortune in heartbreak as well.

him to do, the food rewards are gradually eliminated and only the praise remains. If you were to keep up with the food treats, you could have two problems on your hands—an obese dog and a beggar.

Training begins the minute your Whippet puppy steps through the doorway of your

Ch. Silkstone Jewel in the Crown demonstrates the virtues of good training (and good breeding). This Whippet is a Best in Show winner, owned by Frank and Lee Pieterse.

up to you to reinforce good manners by building on the foundation that you've established. Once your puppy is reliable in basic commands and behavior and has reached the appropriate age, you may gradually introduce him to some of the interesting sports, games and activities available to pet owners and their dogs.

Raising your puppy is a family affair. Each member of the family must know what rules to set forth for the puppy and how to use the same one-word commands to mean exactly the same thing every time. Even if yours is a large family, one person will soon be considered by the pup to be the leader, the Alpha person in his pack, the "boss" who must be obeyed. Often that highly regarded person turns out to be the one who feeds the puppy. Food ranks very high on the puppy's list of important things! That's why your puppy is rewarded with small treats along with verbal praise when he responds to you correctly. As the puppy learns to do what you want

home, so don't make the mistake of putting the puppy on the floor and telling him by your actions to "Go for it! Run wild!" Even if this is your first puppy, you must act as if you know what you're doing: be the boss. An uncertain pup may be terrified to move, while a bold one will be ready to take you at your word and start plotting to destroy the house! Before you collected your puppy, you decided where his own special place would be, and that's where to put him when you first arrive home. Give him a house tour after he has investigated his area and had a nap and a bathroom "pit stop."

It's worth mentioning here that if you've adopted an adult dog that is completely trained to your liking, lucky you! You're off the hook! However, if that dog spent his life up to this point in a kennel, or even in a good home but without any real training, be prepared to tackle the job ahead. A dog three years of age or older with no previous training cannot be blamed for not knowing what he was never taught. While the dog is trying to understand and learn your rules, at the same time he has to unlearn many of his previously self-taught habits and general view of the world.

Working with a professional trainer will speed up your progress with an adopted adult dog. You'll need patience, too.

TEACHER'S PET

Dogs are individuals, not robots, with many traits basic to their breed. Some, bred to work alone, are independent thinkers; others rely on you to call the shots. If you have enrolled in a training class, your instructor can offer alternative methods of training based on your individual dog's instincts and personality. You may benefit from using a different type of collar or switching to a class with different kinds of dogs.

Some new rules may be close to impossible for the dog to accept. After all, he's been successful so far by doing everything his way! (Patience again.) He may agree with your instruction for a few days and then slip back into his old ways, so you must be just as consistent and understanding in your teaching as you would be with a puppy. (More patience needed yet again!) Your dog has to learn to pay attention to your voice, your family, the daily routine, new smells, new sounds and, in some cases, even a new climate.

One of the most important things to find out about a newly adopted adult dog is his reaction to children (yours and others), strangers and your friends, and how he acts upon meeting other dogs. If he was not socialized with dogs as a puppy, this could be a major problem. This does not mean that he's a "bad" dog, a vicious dog or an aggressive dog; rather, it means that he has no idea how to read another dog's body language. There's no way for him to tell whether the other dog is a friend or foe. Survival instinct takes over, telling him to attack first and ask questions later. This definitely calls for professional help and, even then, may not be a behavior that can be corrected 100% reliably (or even at all). If you have a puppy, this is why it is so very important to introduce

THE BEST INVESTMENT
Obedience school is as important for you and your dog as grammar school is for your kids, and it's a lot more fun! Don't shun classes thinking that your dog might embarrass you. He might! Instructors don't expect you to know everything, but they'll teach you the correct way to teach your dog so he won't embarrass you again. He'll become a social animal as you learn with other people and dogs. Home training, while effective in teaching your dog the basic commands, excludes these socialization benefits.

With time, your Whippet will learn whether his walks are recreational or strictly for potty purposes.

your young puppy properly to other puppies and "dog-friendly" adult dogs.

HOUSE-TRAINING

Dogs are tactility-oriented when it comes to house-training. In other words, they respond to the surface on which they are given approval to eliminate. The choice is yours (the dog's version is in parentheses): The lawn (including the neighbors' lawns)? A bare patch of earth under a tree (where people like to sit and relax in the summertime)? Concrete steps or patio (all sidewalks, garages and basement floors)? The curbside (watch out for cars)? A small area of crushed stone in a corner of the yard (mine!)? The latter is the best

choice if you can manage it, because it will remain strictly for the dog's use and is easy to keep clean.

You can start out with paper-training indoors and switch over to an outdoor surface as the puppy matures and gains control over his need to eliminate. For the nay-sayers, don't worry—this won't mean that the dog will soil on every piece of newspaper lying around the house. You are training him to go outside, remember? Starting out by paper-training often is the only choice for a city dog.

LEASH TRAINING

House-training and leash training go hand in hand, literally. When taking your puppy outside to do his business, lead him there on his leash. Unless an emergency potty run is called for, do not whisk the puppy up into your arms and take him outside. If you have a fenced yard, you have the advantage of letting the puppy loose to go out, but it's better to put the dog on the leash and take him to his designated place in the yard until he is reliably house-trained. Taking the puppy for a walk is the best way to house-train a dog. The dog will associate the walk with his time to relieve himself, and the exercise of walking stimulates the dog's bowels and bladder. Dogs that are not trained to relieve themselves on a walk may hold it until they get back home, which of course defeats half the purpose of the walk.

WHEN YOUR PUPPY'S "GOT TO GO"

Your puppy's need to relieve himself is seemingly non-stop, but signs of improvement will be seen each week. From 8 to 10 weeks old, the puppy will have to be taken outside every time he wakes up, about 10–15 minutes after every meal and after every period of play—all day long, from first thing in the morning until his bedtime! That's a total of ten or more trips per day to teach the puppy where it's okay to relieve himself. With that schedule in mind, you can see that house-training a young puppy is not a part-time job. It requires someone to be home all day.

If that seems overwhelming or impossible, do a little planning. For example, plan to pick up your puppy at the start of a vacation period. If you can't get home in the middle of the day, plan to hire a dog-sitter or ask a neighbor to come over to take the pup outside, feed him his lunch and then take him out again about ten or so minutes after he's eaten. Also make arrangements with that or another person to be your "emergency" contact if you have to stay late on the job. Remind yourself—repeatedly—that this hectic schedule improves as the puppy gets older.

HOME WITHIN A HOME

Your Whippet puppy needs to be confined to one secure, puppy-

DAILY SCHEDULE

How many relief trips does your puppy need per day? A puppy up to the age of 14 weeks will need to go outside about 8 to 12 times per day! You will have to take the pup out any time he starts sniffing around the floor or turning in small circles, as well as after naps, meals, games and lessons or whenever he's released from his crate. Once the puppy is 14 to 22 weeks of age, he will require only 6 to 8 relief trips. At the ages of 22 to 32 weeks, the puppy will require about 5 to 7 trips. Adult dogs typically require 4 relief trips per day, in the morning, afternoon, evening and late at night.

proof area when no one is able to watch his every move. Generally the kitchen is the place of choice because the floor is washable. Likewise, it's a busy family area that will accustom the pup to a

POTTY COMMAND

Most dogs love to please their masters; there are no bounds to what dogs will do to make their owners happy. The potty command is a good example of this theory. If toileting on command makes the master happy, then more power to him. Puppies will obligingly piddle if it really makes their keepers smile. Some owners can be creative about which word they will use to command their dogs to relieve themselves. Some popular choices are "Potty," "Tinkle," "Piddle," "Let's go," "Hurry up" and "Toilet." Give the command every time your puppy goes into position and the puppy will begin to associate his business with the command, which will be helpful for the potty routine throughout his life.

critical when you burn something). An exercise pen (also called an "ex-pen," a puppy version of a playpen) within the room of choice is an excellent means of confinement for a young pup. He can see out and has a certain amount of space in which to run about, but he is safe from dangerous things like electrical cords, heating units, trash baskets or open kitchen-supply cabinets. Place the pen where the puppy will not get a blast of heat or air conditioning.

In the pen, you can put a few toys, his bed (which can be his crate if the dimensions of pen and crate are compatible) and a few layers of newspaper in one small corner, just in case. A water bowl can be hung at a convenient height on the side of the ex-pen so it won't become a splashing pool for an innovative puppy. His food dish can go on the floor, near but not under the water bowl.

Crates are something that pet owners are at last getting used to for their dogs. Wild or domestic canines have always preferred to sleep in den-like safe spots, and that is exactly what the crate provides. How often have you seen adult dogs that choose to sleep under a table or chair even though they have full run of the house? It's the den connection.

In your "happy" voice, use the word "Crate" every time you put the pup into his den. If he's new

variety of noises, everything from pots and pans to the telephone, blender and dishwasher. He will also be enchanted by the smell of your cooking (and will never be

Whippets can be a tad clannish and keep secrets from their human pack members.

to a crate, toss in a small biscuit for him to chase the first few times. At night, after he's been outside, he should sleep in his crate. The crate may be kept in his designated area at night or, if you want to be sure to hear those wake-up yips in the morning, put the crate in a corner of your bedroom. However, don't make any response whatsoever to whining or crying. If he's completely ignored, he'll settle down and get to sleep.

Good bedding for a young puppy is an old folded bath towel or an old blanket, something that is easily washable and disposable if necessary ("accidents" will happen!). Never put newspaper in the puppy's crate. Also those old ideas about adding a clock to replace his mother's heartbeat, or a hot-water bottle to replace her warmth, are just that—old ideas. The clock could drive the puppy nuts, and the hot-water bottle could end up as a very soggy waterbed! An extremely good breeder would have introduced your puppy to the crate by letting two pups sleep together for a couple of nights, followed by several nights alone. How thankful you will be if you found that breeder!

Safe toys in the pup's crate or area will keep him occupied, but monitor their condition closely. Discard any toys that show signs

Once reliably trained, your Whippet should go into his crate without much coaxing and will enjoy resting there as a place of safe confinement wherever you go.

of being chewed to bits. Squeaky parts, bits of stuffing or plastic or any other small pieces can cause intestinal blockage or possibly choking if swallowed.

PROGRESSING WITH POTTY-TRAINING
After you've taken your puppy out and he has relieved himself in the area you've selected, he can have some free time with the family as long as there is someone

---

EXTRA! EXTRA!
The headlines read: "Puppy Piddles Here!" Breeders commonly use newspapers to line their whelping pens, so puppies learn to associate newspapers with relieving themselves. Do not use newspapers to line your pup's crate, as this will signal to your puppy that it is OK to urinate in his crate. If you choose to paper-train your puppy, you will layer newspapers on a section of the floor near the door he uses to go outside. You should encourage the puppy to use the papers to relieve himself, and bring him there whenever you see him getting ready to go. Little by little, you will reduce the size of the newspaper-covered area so that the puppy will learn to relieve himself "on the other side of the door."

---

responsible for watching him. That doesn't mean just someone in the same room who is watching TV or busy on the computer, but one person who is doing nothing other than keeping an eye on the pup, playing with him on the floor and helping him understand his position in the pack.

This first taste of freedom will let you begin to set the house rules. If you don't want the dog on the furniture, now is the time to prevent his first attempts to jump up onto the couch. The word to use in this case is "Off," not "Down." "Down" is the word you will use to teach the down position, which is something entirely different.

Most corrections at this stage come in the form of simply distracting the puppy. Instead of telling him "No" for "Don't chew the carpet," distract the chomping puppy with a toy and he'll forget about the carpet.

As you are playing with the pup, do not forget to watch him closely and pay attention to his

SOMEBODY TO BLAME

House-training a puppy can be frustrating for the puppy and the owner alike. The puppy does not instinctively understand the difference between defecating on the pavement outside and on the ceramic tile in the kitchen. He is confused and frightened by his human's exuberant reactions to his natural urges. The owner, arguably the more intelligent of the duo, is also frustrated that he cannot convince his puppy to obey his commands and instructions.

In frustration, the owner may struggle with the temptation to discipline the puppy, scold him or even strike him on the rear end. Shouting and smacking the puppy may make you feel better, but it will defeat your purpose in gaining your puppy's trust and respect. Don't blame your nine-week-old puppy. Blame yourself for not being 100% consistent in the puppy's lessons and routine. The lesson here is simple: try harder and your puppy will succeed.

body language. Whenever you see him begin to circle or sniff, take the puppy outside to relieve himself. If you are paper-training, put him back into his confined area on the newspapers. In either case, praise him as he eliminates while he actually is in the act of relieving himself. Three seconds after he has finished is too late! You'll be praising him for running toward you, or picking up a toy or whatever he may be doing at that moment, and that's not what you

Whippets look up to their owners for approval and guidance.

CANINE DEVELOPMENT SCHEDULE

It is important to understand how and at what age a puppy develops into adulthood.
If you are a puppy owner, consult the following Canine Development Schedule to
determine the stage of development your puppy is currently experiencing.
This knowledge will help you as you work with the puppy in the weeks and months ahead.

PERIOD	AGE	CHARACTERISTICS
FIRST TO THIRD	BIRTH TO SEVEN WEEKS	Puppy needs food, sleep and warmth and responds to simple and gentle touching. Needs mother for security and disciplining. Needs littermates for learning and interacting with other dogs. Pup learns to function within a pack and learns pack order of dominance. Begin socializing pup with adults and children for short periods. Pup begins to become aware of his environment.
FOURTH	EIGHT TO TWELVE WEEKS	Brain is fully developed. Pup needs socializing with outside world. Remove from mother and littermates. Needs to change from canine pack to human pack. Human dominance necessary. Fear period occurs between 8 and 12 weeks. Avoid fright and pain.
FIFTH	THIRTEEN TO SIXTEEN WEEKS	Training and formal obedience should begin. Less association with other dogs, more with people, places, situations. Period will pass easily if you remember this is pup's change-to-adolescence time. Be firm and fair. Flight instinct prominent. Permissiveness and over-disciplining can do permanent damage. Praise for good behavior.
JUVENILE	FOUR TO EIGHT MONTHS	Another fear period about 7 to 8 months of age. It passes quickly, but be cautious of fright and pain. Sexual maturity reached. Dominant traits established. Dog should understand sit, down, come and stay by now.

NOTE: THESE ARE APPROXIMATE TIME FRAMES. ALLOW FOR INDIVIDUAL DIFFERENCES IN PUPPIES.

want to be praising him for. Timing is a vital tool in all dog training. Use it.

Remove soiled newspapers immediately and replace them with clean ones. You may want to take a small piece of soiled paper and place it in the middle of the new clean papers, as the scent will attract him to that spot when it's time to go again. That scent attraction is why it's so important to clean up any messes made in the house by using a product specially made to elimi-

LEADER OF THE PACK

Canines are pack animals. They live according to pack rules, and every pack has only one leader. Guess what? That's you! To establish your position of authority, lay down the rules and be fair and good-natured in all your dealings with your dog. He will consider young children as his littermates, but the one who trains him, who feeds him, who grooms him, who expects him to come into line, that's his leader. And he who leads must be obeyed.

Dog training is a matter of dedication, repetition and communication. If your Whippet will look you in the eye, he is ready and willing to learn.

the leash on quickly and lead him to his spot. Now comes the hard part—hard for you, that is. Just stand there until he urinates and defecates. Move him a few feet in one direction or another if he's just sitting there looking at you, but remember that this is neither playtime nor time for a walk. This is strictly a business trip! Then, as he circles and squats (remember your timing!), give him a quiet "Good dog" as praise. If you start to jump for joy, ecstatic over his performance, he'll do one of two things: either he will stop midstream, as it were, or he'll do it again for you—in the house—and expect you to be just as delighted!

Give him five minutes or so and, if he doesn't go in that time,

Don't get into the habit of carrying your pup to his relief area or he won't learn to go there on his own.

nate the odor of dog urine and droppings. Regular household cleansers won't do the trick. Pet shops sell the best pet deodorizers. Invest in a large container—you will use it.

Scent attraction eventually will lead your pup to his chosen spot outdoors; this is the basis of outdoor training. When you take your puppy outside to relieve himself, use a one-word command such as "Outside" or "Go-potty" (that's one word to the puppy!) as you pick him up and attach his leash. Then put him down in his area. If for any reason you can't carry him, snap

---

BASIC PRINCIPLES OF DOG TRAINING

1. Start training early. A young puppy is ready, willing and able.
2. Timing is your all-important tool. Praise at the exact time that the dog responds correctly. Pay close attention.
3. Patience is almost as important as timing!
4. Repeat! The same word has to mean the same thing every time.
5. In the beginning, praise all correct behavior verbally, along with treats and petting.

outdoors immediately. No punishment is needed. You and your puppy are just learning each other's language, and sometimes it's easy to miss a puppy's message. Chalk it up to experience and watch more closely from now on.

KEEPING THE PACK ORDERLY

Discipline is a form of training that brings order to life. For example, military discipline is what allows the soldiers in an army to work as one. Discipline is a form of teaching and, in dogs, is the basis of how the successful pack operates. Each member knows his place in the pack and all respect the leader, or Alpha dog. It is essential for your puppy that you establish this type of relationship, with you as the Alpha, or leader. It is a form of social coexistence that all canines recognize and accept. Discipline, therefore, is

take him back indoors to his confined area and try again in another ten minutes, or immediately if you see him sniffing and circling. By careful observation, you'll soon work out a successful schedule.

Accidents, by the way, are just that—accidents. Clean them up quickly and thoroughly, without comment, after the puppy has been taken outside to finish his business and then put back into his area or crate. If you witness an accident in progress, say "No!" in a stern voice and get the pup

Whippets truly enjoy each other's company and do well in multiple-pet homes. In fact, a well-trained dog can serve as an example for another's good behavior!

and swallow, providing instant positive reinforcement. If he has to take time to chew a big crunchy dog treat, he will have forgotten what he did to earn it by the time he is finished.

Your puppy should never be physically punished. The displeasure shown on your face and in your voice is sufficient to signal to the pup that he has done something wrong. He wants to please everyone higher up on the social ladder, especially his leader, so a scowl and harsh voice will take care of the error. Growling out the word "Shame!" when the pup is

Teaching a dog to stay in the standing position, necessary for show dogs, requires the dog to have discipline and focus.

never to be confused with punishment. When you teach your puppy how you want him to behave, and he behaves properly and you praise him for it, you are disciplining him with a form of positive reinforcement.

For a dog, rewards come in the form of praise, a smile, a cheerful tone of voice, a few friendly pats or a rub of the ears. Rewards are also small food treats. Obviously, that does not mean bits of regular dog food. Instead, treats are very small bits of special things like cheese or pieces of soft dog treats. The idea is to reward the dog with something very small that he can taste

DON'T STRESS ME OUT

Your dog doesn't have to deal with paying the bills, the daily commute, PTA meetings and the like, but, believe it or not, there's lots of stress in a dog's world. Stress can be caused by the owner's impatient demeanor and his angry or harsh corrections. If your dog cringes when you reach for his training collar, he's stressed. An older dog is sometimes stressed out when he goes to a new home. No matter what the cause, put off all training until he's over it. If he's going through a fear period—shying away from people, trembling when spoken to, avoiding eye contact or hiding under furniture—wait to resume training. Naturally you'd also postpone your lessons if the dog were sick, and the same goes for you. Show some compassion.

TIME TO PLAY!

Playtime can happen both indoors and out. A young puppy is growing so rapidly that he needs sleep more than he needs a lot of physical exercise. Puppies get sufficient exercise on their own just through normal puppy activity. Monitor play with young children so you can remove the puppy when he's had enough, or calm the kids if they get too rowdy. Almost all puppies love to chase after a toy you've thrown, and you can turn your games into educational activities. Every time your puppy brings the toy back to you, say "Give it" (or "Drop it") followed by "Good dog" and throwing it again. If he's reluctant to give it to you, offer a small treat so that he drops the toy as he takes the treat. He will soon get the idea.

caught in the act of doing something wrong is better than the repetitive "No." Some dogs hear "No" so often that they begin to think it's their name! By the way, do not use the dog's name when you're correcting him. His name is reserved to get his attention for something pleasant about to take place.

There are punishments that have nothing to do with you. For example, your dog may think that chasing cats is one reason for his existence. You can try to stop it as much as you like but without success, because it's such fun for the dog. But one good hissing,

spitting, swipe of a cat's claws across the dog's nose will put an end to the game forever. Intervene only when your dog's eyeball is seriously at risk. Cat scratches can cause permanent damage to an innocent but annoying puppy.

GETTING STARTED

COLLAR AND LEASH

Before you begin your Whippet puppy's education, he must be used to his collar and leash. Choose a collar for your puppy that is secure, but not heavy or bulky. He won't enjoy training if he's uncomfortable. A flat buckle collar is fine for everyday wear and for initial puppy training. For older dogs, there are several types of training collars such as the martingale, which is a double loop that tightens slightly around the neck, or the head collar, which is similar to a horse's halter. Do not use a chain choke collar with your Whippet; the martingale is the recommended training collar for the breed.

A lightweight 6-foot woven cotton or nylon training leash is preferred by most trainers because it is easy to fold up in your hand and comfortable to hold because there is a certain amount of give to it. There are lessons where the dog will start off 6 feet away from you at the end of the leash. The leash used

right way (and the wrong way) to interact with other dogs as well as their people. You cannot teach your puppy how to interpret another dog's sign language. For a first-time puppy owner, these socialization classes are invaluable. For experienced dog owners, they are a real boon to further training.

ATTENTION

You've been using the dog's name since the minute you collected him from the breeder, so you should be able to get his attention by saying his name—with a big smile and in an excited tone of voice. His response will be the puppy equivalent of "Here I am! What are we going to do?" Your immediate response (if you haven't guessed by now) is "Good dog." Rewarding him at the

Once trained, Whippets are consistent and reliable, which are ideal traits for dogs pursuing a show career.

The use of treats is an accepted, effective practice in dog training. The dog is rewarded when he successfully performs a command.

to take the puppy outside to relieve himself is shorter because you don't want him to roam away from his area. The shorter leash will also be the one to use when you walk the puppy.

If you've been wise enough to enroll in a Puppy Kindergarten Training class, suggestions will be made as to the best collar and leash for your young puppy. I say "wise" because your puppy will be in a class with puppies in his age range (up to five months old) of all breeds and sizes. It's the perfect way for him to learn the

moment he pays attention to you teaches him the proper way to respond when he hears his name.

EXERCISES FOR A BASIC CANINE EDUCATION

THE SIT EXERCISE
There are several ways to teach the puppy to sit. The first one is to catch him whenever he is about to sit and, as his backside nears the floor, say "Sit, good dog!" That's positive reinforcement and, if your timing is sharp, he will learn that what he's doing at that second is connected to your saying "Sit" and that you think he's clever for doing it!

Another method is to start with the puppy on his leash in front of you. Show him a treat in the palm of your right hand. Bring your hand up under his nose and, almost in slow motion, move your hand up and back so his nose goes up in the air and his head tilts back as he follows the treat in your hand. At that point, he will have to either sit or fall over, so as his back legs buckle under, say "Sit, good dog," and then give him the treat and lots of praise. You may have to begin with your hand lightly running up his chest, actually lifting his chin up until he sits. Some (usually older) dogs require gentle pressure on their hindquarters with the left hand, in which case the dog should be

on your left side. Puppies generally do not appreciate this physical dominance.

After a few times, you should be able to show the dog a treat in the open palm of your hand, raise your hand waist-high as you say "Sit" and have him sit. Once again, you have taught him two

A SIMPLE "SIT"
When you command your dog to sit, use the word "Sit." Do not say "Sit down," as your dog will not know whether you mean "Sit" or "Down," or maybe you mean both. Be clear in your instructions to your dog; use one-word commands and always be consistent.

If the "follow the treat" method doesn't work, an extra-resistant Whippet may need a little more help into the down position.

I WILL FOLLOW YOU

Obedience isn't just a classroom activity. In your home you have many great opportunities to teach your dog polite manners. Allowing your pet on the bed or furniture elevates him to your level, which is not a good idea (the word is "Off!"). Use the "umbilical cord" method, keeping your dog on lead so he has to go with you wherever you go. You sit, he sits. You walk, he heels. You stop, he sit/stays. Everywhere you go, he's with you, but you go first!

things at the same time. Both the verbal command and the motion of the hand are signals for the sit. Your puppy is watching you almost more than he is listening to you, so what you do is just as important as what you say.

Don't save any of these drills only for training sessions. Use them as much as possible at odd times during a normal day. The dog should always sit before being given his food dish. He should sit to let you go through a doorway first, when the doorbell rings or when you stop to speak to someone on the street.

THE DOWN EXERCISE

Before beginning to teach the down command, you must consider how the dog feels about this exercise. To him, "down" is a submissive position. Being flat on the floor with you standing over him is not his idea of fun. It's up to you to let him know that, while it may not be fun, the reward of your approval is worth his effort.

Start with the puppy on your left side in a sit position. Hold the leash right above his collar in your left hand. Have an extra-special treat, such as a small piece of cooked chicken or hot dog, in your right hand. Place it at the end of the pup's nose and steadily move your hand down and forward along the ground. Hold the leash to prevent a sudden lunge for the food. As the puppy goes into the down position, say "Down" very gently.

The difficulty with this exercise is twofold: it's both the

submissive aspect and the fact that most people say the word "Down" as if they were a drill sergeant in charge of recruits! So issue the command sweetly, give him the treat and have the pup maintain the down position for several seconds. If he tries to get up immediately, place your hands on his shoulders and press down gently, giving him a very quiet "Good dog." As you progress with this lesson, increase the "down time" until he will hold it until you say "Okay" (his cue for release). Practice this one in the house at various times throughout the day.

By increasing the length of time during which the dog must maintain the down position, you'll find many uses for it. For example, he can lie at your feet in the vet's office or anywhere that both of you have to wait, when you are on the phone, while the

OKAY!

This is the signal that tells your dog that he can quit whatever he was doing. Use "Okay" to end a session on a correct response to a command (never end on an incorrect response). Lots of praise follows. People use "Okay" a lot and it has other uses for dogs, too. Your dog is barking. You say, "Okay! Come!" "Okay" signals him to stop the barking activity and "Come" allows him to come to you for a "Good dog."

family is eating and so forth. If you progress to training for competitive obedience, he'll already be all set for the exercise called the "long down."

THE STAY EXERCISE

You can teach your Whippet to stay in the sit, down and stand positions. To teach the sit/stay, have the dog sit on your left side. Hold the leash at waist level in your left hand and let the dog know that you have a treat in your closed right hand. Step forward on your right foot as you say "Stay." Immediately turn and stand directly in front of the dog, keeping your right hand up high so he'll keep his eye on the treat hand and maintain the sit position for a count of five. Return to your original position and offer the reward.

Increase the length of the sit/stay each time until the dog can hold it for at least 30 seconds without moving. After about a week of success, move out on your right foot and take two steps before turning to face the dog. Give the "Stay" hand signal (left palm back toward the dog's head) as you leave. He gets the treat when you return and he holds the sit/stay. Increase the distance that you walk away from him before turning until you reach the length of your training leash. But don't rush it! Go back to the beginning if he moves before he

completely reliable and steady with the down command. Again, don't rush it. With the dog in the down position on your left side, step out on your right foot as you say "Stay." Return by walking around in back of the dog and into your original position. While you are training, it's okay to murmur something like "Hold on" to encourage him to stay put. When the dog will stay without moving when you are at a distance of 3 or 4 feet, begin to increase the length of time before you return. Be sure he holds the down on your return until you say

Be sure the dog is comfortable in the down position before attempting the down/stay.

should. No matter what the lesson, never be upset by having to back up for a few days. The repetition and practice are what will make your dog reliable in these commands. It won't do any good to move on to something more difficult if the command is not mastered at the easier levels. Above all, even if you do get frustrated, never let your puppy know! Always keep a positive, upbeat attitude during training, which will transmit to your dog for positive results.

The down/stay is taught in the same way once the dog is

FEAR AGGRESSION
Of the several types of aggression, the one brought on by fear is the most difficult for people to comprehend and to deal with. Aggression to protect food, or any object the dog perceives as his, is more easily understood. Fear aggression is quite different. The dog shows fear, generally for no apparent reason. He backs off, cowers or hides under the bed. If he's on lead, he will hide behind your leg and lash out unexpectedly. No matter how you approach him, he will bite. A fear-biter attacks with great speed and instantly retreats. Don't shout at him or go near him. Don't coddle, sympathize or try to protect him. To him, that's a reward. As with other forms of aggression, get professional help.

Your Whippet(s) should come running when called. Teaching the come exercise should be an enjoyable time for you and your Whippet.

"Okay." At that point, he gets his treat—just so he'll remember for next time that it's not over until it's over.

SHOULD WE ENROLL?

If you have the means and the time, you should definitely take your dog to obedience classes. Begin with Puppy Kindergarten Classes in which puppies of all sizes learn basic lessons while getting the opportunity to meet and greet each other; it's as much about socialization as it is about good manners. What you learn in class you can practice at home. And if you goof up in practice, you'll get help in the next session.

THE COME EXERCISE

No command is more important to the safety of your Whippet than "Come." It is what you should say every single time you see the puppy running toward you: "Binky, come! Good dog." During playtime, run a few feet away from the puppy and turn and tell him to "Come" as he is already running to you. You can go so far as to teach your puppy two things at once if you squat down and hold out your arms. As the pup gets close to you and you're saying "Good dog," bring your right arm in about waist high. Now he's also learning the hand signal, an excellent device should

leash. This time, catch him off guard, while he's sniffing a leaf or watching a bird: "Binky, come!" You may have to pause for a split second after his name to be sure you have his attention. If the puppy shows any sign of confusion, give the leash a mild jerk and take a couple of steps backward. Do not repeat the command. In this case, you should say "Good come" as he reaches you.

That's the number-one rule of training. Each command word is given just once. Anything more is nagging. You'll also notice that all commands are one word only. Even when they are actually two words, you say them as one.

Never call the dog to come to you—with or without his name—if you are angry or intend to correct him for some misbehavior. When correcting the pup, you go to him. Your dog must always connect "Come" with something

COME AND GET IT!
The come command is your dog's safety signal. Until he is 99% perfect in responding, don't use the come command if you cannot enforce it. Practice on leash with treats or squeakers, or whenever the dog is running to you. Never call him to come to you if he is to be corrected for a misdemeanor. Reward the dog with a treat and happy praise whenever he comes to you.

Only attempt training off lead in a safe area and only if your Whippet is already reliable with the command on lead.

you be on the phone when you need to get him to come to you! You'll also both be one step ahead when you enter obedience classes.

When the puppy responds to your well-timed "Come," try it with the puppy on the training pleasant and with your approval; then you can rely on his response.

Puppies, like children, have notoriously short attention spans, so don't overdo it with any of the training. Keep each lesson short. Break it up with a quick run around the yard or a ball toss, repeat the lesson and quit as soon as the pup gets it right. That way, you will always end with a "Good dog."

Life isn't perfect and neither are puppies. A time will come, often around 10 months of age, when he'll become "selectively deaf" or choose to "forget" his name. He may respond by wagging his tail (and even seeming to smile at you) with a look that says "Make me!" Laugh, throw his favorite toy and skip the lesson you had planned. Pups will be pups!

THE HEEL EXERCISE

The second most important command to teach, after the come, is the heel. When you are walking your growing puppy, you need to be in control. Besides, it looks terrible to be pulled and yanked down the street, and it's not much fun either. Your eight- to ten-week-old puppy will probably follow you everywhere, but that's his natural instinct, not your control over the situation. However, any time he does follow you, you can say "Heel" and be ahead of the game, as he will learn to associate this

RIGHT CLICK ON YOUR DOG

With three clicks, the dolphin jumps through the hoop. Wouldn't it be nice to have a dog who could obey wordless commands that easily? Clicker training actually was developed by dolphin trainers and today is used on dogs with great success. You can buy a clicker at a pet shop or pet-supply outlet, and then you'll be off and clicking.

You can click your dog into learning new commands, shaping or conditioning his behavior and solving bad habits. The clicker, used in conjunction with a treat, is an extension of positive reinforcement. The dog begins to recognize your happy clicking, and that becomes sufficient positive reinforcement. The dog is conditioned to follow your hand with the clicker, just as he would follow your hand with a treat. To discourage the dog from inappropriate behavior (like jumping up or barking), you can use the clicker to set a timeframe and then click and reward the dog once he's waited the allotted time without jumping up or barking.

command with the action of following you before you even begin teaching him to heel.

There is a very precise, almost military, procedure for teaching your dog to heel. As with all other obedience training, begin with the dog on your left

Training the Whippet for agility trials requires patience and experience. This Whippet is learning to "weave."

Walk a few steps and stop while the puppy is correctly beside you. Tell him to sit and give mild verbal praise (more enthusiastic praise will encourage him to think the lesson is over). Repeat the lesson, increasing the number of steps you take only as long as the dog is heeling nicely

A diificult exercise in agility is the extended stay, requiring the dog to stop running and stay for a short period of time.

side. He will be in a very nice sit and you will have the training leash across your chest. Hold the loop and folded leash in your right hand. Pick up the slack leash above the dog in your left hand and hold it loosely at your side. Step out on your left foot as you say "Heel." If the puppy does not move, give a gentle tug or pat your left leg to get him started. If he surges ahead of you, stop and pull him back gently until he is at your side. Tell him to sit and begin again.

beside you. When you end the lesson, have him hold the sit, then give him the "Okay" to let him know that this is the end of the lesson. Praise him so that he knows he did a good job.

The cure for excessive pulling (a common problem) is to stop when the dog is no more than 2 or 3 feet ahead of you. Guide him back into position and begin again. With a really determined puller, try switching to a head collar. This will automatically turn the pup's head toward you so you can bring him back easily to the heel position. Give quiet, reassuring praise every time the leash goes slack and he's staying with you.

Staying and heeling can take a lot out of a dog, so provide playtime and free-running exercise to shake off the stress when the lessons are over. You don't want

him to associate training with all work and no fun.

TAPERING OFF TIDBITS

Your dog has been watching you—and the hand that treats—throughout all of his lessons, and now it's time to break the treat habit. Begin by giving him treats at the end of each lesson only. Then start to give a treat after the end of only some of the lessons. At the end of every lesson, as well as during the lessons, be consistent with the praise. Your pup now doesn't know whether he'll get a treat or not, but he should keep performing well just in case! Finally, you will stop giving treat rewards entirely. Save them for something brand-new that you want to teach him. Keep up the praise and you'll always have a "good dog."

OBEDIENCE CLASSES

The advantages of an obedience class are that your dog will have

Through the collapsible tunnel, this Whippet is flying toward the finish.

Training for the extended stay; in an actual agility trial, the dog stays in the down on a platform.

Garbed in his racing silk, this Whippet is living up to the breed's appellation, windhound.

your own. You will also learn all of the requirements for competitive obedience trials, in which you can earn titles and go on to advanced jumping and retrieving exercises, which are fun for many dogs. Obedience classes build the foundation needed for many other canine activities (in which we humans are allowed to participate, too!).

to learn amid the distractions of other people and dogs and that your mistakes will be quickly corrected by the trainer. Teaching your dog along with a qualified instructor and other handlers who may have more dog experience than you is another plus of the class environment. The instructor and other handlers can help you to find the most efficient way of teaching your dog a command or exercise. It's often easier to learn by other people's mistakes than

TRAINING FOR OTHER ACTIVITIES
Once your dog has basic obedience under his collar and is 12 months of age, you can enter the world of agility training. Dogs think agility is pure fun, like being turned loose in an amusement park full of obstacles! In addition to competitive obedience and agility, there are lure-coursing and racing events for sighthounds, and tracking, which is open to all "nosey" dogs (which would include all dogs!).

Whippet races make exciting outings for dogs and their owners. There's much enjoyment for owners to watch their dogs fulfill their calling.

Your quick and agile sighthound is well-suited to traditional pursuits of racing and lure coursing. Whippets do not participate in races with larger sighthound breeds (like the Greyhound, Saluki and Irish Wolfhound). The Whippet Racing Association and its affiliates govern Whippet racing. In addition, the Whippet has much potential in agility competition. On the flipside, this quick, athletic breed is also extremely gentle and makes a wonderful therapy dog. For those who like to volunteer, there is the wonderful feeling of owning a therapy dog and visiting

HOW DO I GET TO CARNEGIE HALL?

Or the National Obedience Championships? The same way you get your dog to do anything else—practice, practice, practice. It's *how* you practice that counts. Keep sessions short, varied, interesting and interspersed with active fun. A bored dog isn't learning. If you're feeling out of sorts yourself, quit for the day. Set yourself a reasonable schedule for several brief practice sessions every day and stick to it. Practice randomly throughout the day as you're doing different things around the house. Lots of praise for that good "Sit" in front of the TV or while waiting for his dinner!

hospices, nursing homes and veterans' homes to bring smiles, comfort and companionship to those who live there.

Around the house, your Whippet can be taught to do some simple chores. You might teach him to carry a basket of household items or to fetch the morning newspaper. The kids can teach the dog all kinds of tricks, from playing hide-and-seek to balancing a biscuit on his nose. A family dog is what rounds out the family. Everything he does beyond sitting in your lap or gazing lovingly at you represents the bonus of owning a dog.

The results of your training efforts are a well-behaved dog, a happy owner and a wonderful friendship.

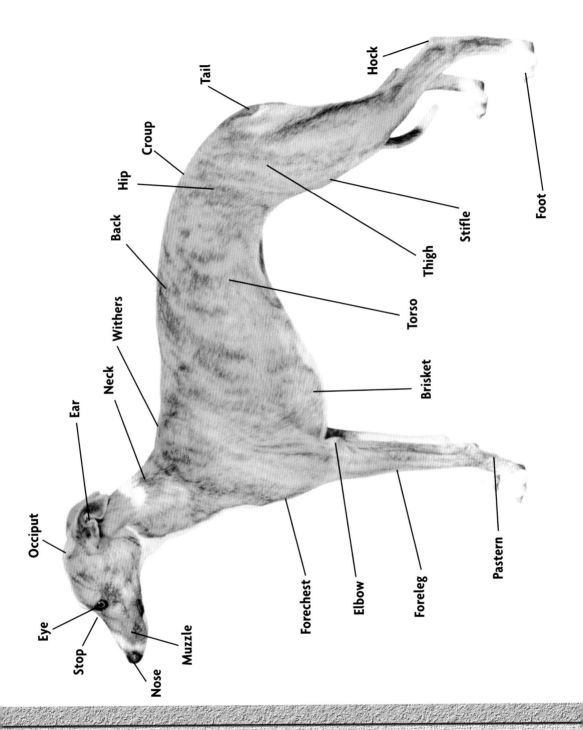

PHYSICAL STRUCTURE OF THE WHIPPET

Tail

Hock

Croup

Hip

Foot

Back

Stifle

Thigh

Withers

Neck

Torso

Ear

Brisket

Occiput

Eye

Forechest

Stop

Elbow

Nose

Foreleg

Muzzle

Pastern

WHIPPET

By Lowell Ackerman DVM, DACVD

HEALTHCARE FOR A LIFETIME

When you own a dog, you become his healthcare advocate over his entire lifespan, as well as being the one to shoulder the financial burden of such care. Accordingly, it is worthwhile to focus on prevention rather than treatment, as you and your pet will both be happier.

Of course, the best place to have begun your program of preventive healthcare is with the initial purchase or adoption of your dog. There is no way of guaranteeing that your new four-legged friend is free of medical problems, but there are some things you can do to improve your odds. You certainly should have done adequate research into the Whippet and have selected your puppy carefully rather than buying on impulse. Health issues aside, a large number of pet abandonment and relinquishment cases arise from a mismatch between pet needs and owner expectations. This is entirely preventable with appropriate planning and finding a good breeder.

Regarding healthcare issues specifically, it is very difficult to make blanket statements about where to acquire a problem-free pet, but, again, a reputable breeder is your best bet. In an ideal situation, you have the opportunity to see both parents, get references from other owners of the breeder's pups and see genetic-testing documentation for several generations of the litter's ancestors. At the very least, you must thoroughly investigate your breed of interest and the problems inherent in that breed, as well as the genetic testing available to screen for those problems. Genetic testing offers some important benefits, but testing is available for only

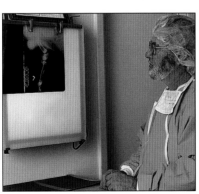

Before you buy a dog, meet and interview the veterinarians in your area. Take everything into consideration; discuss background, specialties, fees, emergency policies, experience with the breed, and so forth.

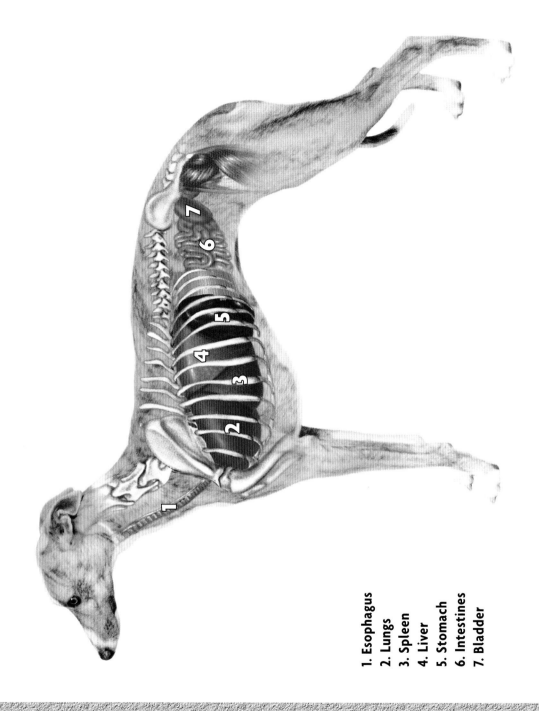

1. Esophagus
2. Lungs
3. Spleen
4. Liver
5. Stomach
6. Intestines
7. Bladder

INTERNAL ORGANS OF THE WHIPPET

a few disorders in a relatively small number of breeds and is not available for some of the most common genetic diseases, such as hip dysplasia, cataracts, epilepsy, cardiomyopathy, etc. This area of research is indeed exciting and increasingly important, and advances will continue to be made each year. In fact, recent research has shown that there is an equivalent dog gene for 75% of known human genes, so research done in either species is likely to benefit the other.

We've also discussed that evaluating the behavioral nature of your Whippet and that of his immediate family members is an important part of the selection process that cannot be underesti-mated or overemphasized. It is sometimes difficult to evaluate temperament in puppies because certain behavioral tendencies, such as some forms of aggression, may not be immediately evident. More dogs are euthanized each year for behavioral reasons than for all medical conditions combined, so it is critical to take temperament issues seriously. Start with a well-balanced, friendly companion and put the time and effort into proper socialization, and you will both be rewarded with a lifelong valued relationship.

Assuming that you have started off with a pup from healthy, sound stock, you then become responsible for helping your veterinarian keep your pet healthy. Some crucial things happen before you even bring your puppy home. Parasite control typically begins at two weeks of age, and vaccinations typically begin at six to eight weeks of age. A pre-pubertal evaluation is typically scheduled for about six months of age. At this time, a dental evaluation is done (since the adult teeth are now in), heartworm prevention is started and neutering or spaying is most commonly done.

It is critical to commence regular dental care at home if you have not already done so. It may not sound very important, but most dogs have active periodontal disease by four years of age if they don't have their teeth cleaned

ANESTHESIA DANGERS

Due to the Whippet's extreme low body fat, anesthesia can be very dangerous for this breed, even for the most routine procedures. Discuss this danger with your vet.

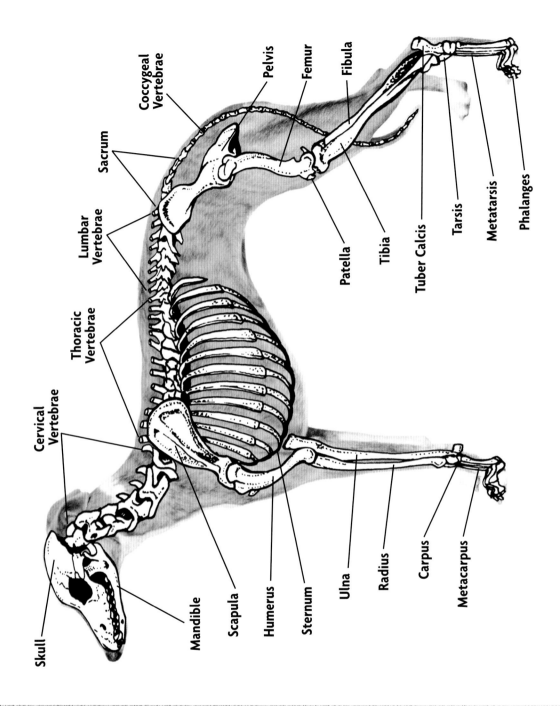

Coccygeal Vertebrae

Pelvis

Femur

Fibula

Sacrum

Patella

Tibia

Tuber Calcis

Tarsis

Metatarsis

Phalanges

Lumbar Vertebrae

Thoracic Vertebrae

Cervical Vertebrae

Skull

Mandible

Scapula

Humerus

Sternum

Ulna

Radius

Carpus

Metacarpus

SKELETAL STRUCTURE OF THE WHIPPET

regularly at home, not just at their veterinary exams. Dental problems lead to more than just bad "doggie breath": gum disease can have very serious medical consequences. If you start brushing your dog's teeth and using antiseptic rinses from a young age, your dog will be accustomed to it and will not resist. The results will be healthy dentition, which your pet will need to enjoy a long, healthy life.

Most dogs are considered adults at a year of age, although

TAKING YOUR DOG'S TEMPERATURE

It is important to know how to take your dog's temperature at times when you think he may be ill. It's not the most enjoyable task, but it can be done without too much difficulty. It's easier with a helper, preferably someone with whom the dog is friendly, so that one of you can hold the dog while the other inserts the thermometer.

Before inserting the thermometer, coat the end with petroleum jelly. Insert the thermometer slowly and gently into the dog's rectum about one inch. Wait for the reading, about two minutes. Be sure to remove the thermometer carefully and clean it thoroughly after each use.

A dog's normal body temperature is between 100.5 and 102.5 degrees F. Immediate veterinary attention is required if the dog's temperature is below 99 or above 104 degrees F.

some larger breeds still have some filling out to do up to about two or so years old. Even individual dogs within each breed have different healthcare requirements, so work with your veterinarian to determine what will be needed and what your role should be. This doctor-client relationship is important, because as vaccination guidelines change, there may not be an annual "vaccine visit" scheduled. You must make sure that you see your veterinarian at least annually, even if no vaccines are due, because this is the best opportunity to coordinate healthcare activities and to make sure that no medical issues creep by unaddressed.

When your Whippet reaches three-quarters of his anticipated lifespan, he is considered a "senior" and likely requires some special care. In general, if you've been taking great care of your canine companion throughout his formative and adult years, the transition to senior status should be a smooth one. Age is not a disease, and as long as everything is functioning as it should, there is no reason why most of late adulthood should not be rewarding for both you and your pet. This is especially true if you have tended to the details, such as regular veterinary visits, proper dental care, excellent nutrition and management of bone and joint issues.

At this stage in your Whippet's life, your veterinarian may want to

EAR CARE

Not every dog's ears are the same. Ears that are open to the air are healthier than ears with poor air circulation. Sometimes a dog can have two differently shaped ears. You should not probe inside your dog's ears. Only clean that which is accessible with a soft cotton wipe; do not use a cotton swab, as this could cause injury if you delve too deeply or if the dog fidgets.

schedule visits twice yearly, instead of once, to run some laboratory screenings, electrocardiograms and the like, and to change the diet to something more digestible. Catching problems early is the best way to manage them effectively. Treating the early stages of heart disease is so much easier than trying to intervene when there is more significant damage to the heart muscle. Similarly, managing the beginning of kidney problems is fairly routine if there is no significant kidney damage. Other problems, like cognitive dysfunction (similar to senility and Alzheimer's disease), cancer,

diabetes and arthritis, are more common in older dogs, but all can be treated to help the dog live as many happy, comfortable years as possible. Just as in people, medical management is more effective (and less expensive) when you catch things early.

SELECTING A VETERINARIAN
There is probably no more important decision that you will make regarding your pet's healthcare than the selection of his doctor. Your pet's veterinarian will be a pediatrician, family-practice physician and gerontologist, depending on the dog's life stage, and will be the individual who makes recommendations regarding issues such as when specialists need to be consulted, when diagnostic testing and/or therapeutic intervention is needed and when you will need to seek outside emergency and critical-care services. Your vet will act as your advocate and liaison throughout these processes.

Everyone has his own idea about what to look for in a vet, an individual who will play a big role in his dog's (and, of course, his own) life for many years to come. For some, it is the compassionate caregiver with whom they hope to develop a professional relationship to span the lifetime of their dogs and even their future pets. For others, they are seeking a clinician with keen diagnostic and therapeutic insight who can deliver state-of-the-art healthcare. Still others need a veterinary facility that is open evenings and weekends, or is in close proximity or provides mobile veterinary services, to accommodate their schedules; these people may not much mind that their dogs might see different veterinarians on each visit.

Just as we have different reasons for selecting our own healthcare professionals (e.g., covered by insurance plan, expert in field, convenient location, etc.), we should not expect that there is a one-size-fits-all recommendation for selecting a veterinarian and veterinary practice. The best advice is to be honest in your assessment of what you expect from a veterinary practice and to conscientiously research the options in your area. You will quickly appreciate that not all veterinary practices are the same, and you will be happiest with one that truly meets your needs.

There is another point to be considered in the selection of veterinary services. Not that long ago, a single veterinarian would attempt to manage all medical and surgical issues as they arose. That was often problematic, because veterinarians are trained in many species and many diseases, and it was just impossible for general veterinary practitioners to be experts in every species, every

---

YOUR DOG NEEDS TO VISIT THE VET IF:

- He has ingested a toxin such as antifreeze or a toxic plant; in these cases, administer first aid and call the vet right away
- His teeth are discolored, loose or missing or he has sores or other signs of infection or abnormality in the mouth
- He has been vomiting, has had diarrhea or has been constipated for over 24 hours; call immediately if you notice blood
- He has refused food for over 24 hours
- His eating habits, water intake or toilet habits have noticeably changed; if you have noticed weight gain or weight loss
- He shows symptoms of bloat, which requires *immediate* attention (discuss this with your vet so you know how to recognize the signs)
- He is salivating excessively
- He has a lump in his throat
- He has a lumps or bumps anywhere on the body
- He is very lethargic
- He appears to be in pain or otherwise has trouble chewing or swallowing
- His skin loses elasticity

Of course, there will be other instances in which a visit to the vet is necessary; these are just some of the signs that could be indicative of serious problems that need to be caught as early as possible.

breed, every field and every ailment. However, just as in the human healthcare fields, specialization has allowed general practitioners to concentrate on primary healthcare delivery, especially wellness and the prevention of infectious diseases, and to utilize a network of specialists to assist in the management of conditions that require specific expertise and experience. Thus there are now many types of veterinary specialists, including dermatologists, cardiologists, ophthalmologists, surgeons, internists, oncologists, neurologists, behaviorists, criticalists and others to help primary-care veterinarians deal with complicated medical challenges. In most cases, specialists see cases referred by primary-care veterinarians, make diagnoses and set up management plans. From there, the animals' ongoing care is returned to their primary-care veterinarians. This important team approach to your pet's medical-care needs has provided opportunities for advanced care and an unparalleled level of quality to be delivered.

With all of the opportunities for your Whippet to receive high-quality veterinary medical care, there is another topic that needs to be addressed at the same time—cost. It's been said that you can have excellent healthcare or inexpensive healthcare, but never both; this is as true in veterinary medicine as it is in human medicine. While veterinary costs are a fraction of what the same services cost in the human healthcare arena, it is still difficult to deal with unanticipated medical costs, especially since they can easily creep into hundreds or even thousands of dollars if specialists or emergency services become involved. However, there are ways of managing these risks. The easiest is to buy pet health insurance and realize that its foremost purpose is not to cover routine healthcare visits but rather to serve as an umbrella for those rainy days when your pet needs medical care and you don't want to worry about whether or not you can afford that care.

Pet insurance policies are very cost-effective (and very inexpensive by human health-insurance standards), but make sure that you buy the policy long before you intend to use it (preferably starting in puppyhood, because coverage will exclude pre-existing conditions) and that you are actually buying an indemnity insurance plan from an insurance company that is regulated by your state or province. Many insurance policy look-alikes are actually discount clubs that are redeemable only at specific locations and for specific services. An indemnity plan covers your pet at almost all veterinary, specialty and emergency practices and is an excellent way to manage your pet's ongoing healthcare needs.

VACCINATIONS AND INFECTIOUS DISEASES

There has never been an easier time to prevent a variety of infectious diseases in your dog, but the advances we've made in veterinary medicine come with a price—choice. Now while it may seem that choice is a good thing (and it is), it has never been more difficult for the pet owner (or the veterinarian) to make an informed decision about the best way to protect pets through vaccination.

Years ago, it was just accepted that puppies got a starter series of vaccinations and then annual "boosters" throughout their lives to keep them protected. As more and more vaccines became available, consumers wanted the convenience of having all of that protection in a single injection. The result was "multivalent" vaccines that crammed a lot of protection into a single syringe. The manufacturers' recommendations were to give the vaccines annually, and this was a simple enough protocol to follow. However, as veterinary medicine has become more sophisticated and we have started looking more at healthcare quandaries rather than convenience, it became

SAMPLE VACCINATION SCHEDULE

6–8 weeks of age	Parvovirus, Distemper, Adenovirus-2 (Hepatitis)
9–11 weeks of age	Parvovirus, Distemper, Adenovirus-2 (Hepatitis)
12–14 weeks of age	Parvovirus, Distemper, Adenovirus-2 (Hepatitis)
16–20 weeks of age	Rabies
1 year of age	Parvovirus, Distemper, Adenovirus-2 (Hepatitis), Rabies

Revaccination is performed every one to three years, depending on the product, the method of administration and the patient's risk. Initial adult inoculation (for dogs at least 16 weeks of age in which a puppy series was not done or could not be confirmed) is two vaccinations, done three to four weeks apart, with revaccination according to the same criteria mentioned. Other vaccines are given as decided between owner and veterinarian.

COMMON INFECTIOUS DISEASES

Let's discuss some of the diseases that create the need for vaccination in the first place. Following are the major canine infectious diseases and a simple explanation of each.

Rabies: A devastating viral disease that can be fatal in dogs and people. In fact, vaccination of dogs and cats is an important public-health measure to create a resistant animal buffer population to protect people from contracting the disease. Vaccination schedules are determined on a government level and are not optional for pet owners; rabies vaccination is required by law in all 50 states.

Parvovirus: A severe, potentially life-threatening disease that is easily transmitted between dogs. There are four strains of the virus, but it is believed that there is significant "cross-protection" between strains that may be included in individual vaccines.

Distemper: A potentially severe and life-threatening disease with a relatively high risk of exposure, especially in certain regions. In very high-risk distemper environments, young pups may be vaccinated with human measles vaccine, a related virus that offers cross-protection when administered at four to ten weeks of age.

Hepatitis: Caused by canine adenovirus type 1 (CAV-1), but since vaccination with the causative virus has a higher rate of adverse effects, cross-protection is derived from the use of adenovirus type 2 (CAV-2), a cause of respiratory disease and one of the potential causes of canine cough. Vaccination with CAV-2 provides long-term immunity against hepatitis, but relatively less protection against respiratory infection.

Canine cough: Also called tracheobronchitis, actually a fairly complicated result of viral and bacterial offenders; therefore, even with vaccination, protection is incomplete. Wherever dogs congregate, canine cough will likely be spread among them. Intranasal vaccination with *Bordetella* and parainfluenza is the best safeguard, but the duration of immunity does not appear to be very long, typically a year at most. These are non-core vaccines, but vaccination is sometimes mandated by boarding kennels, obedience classes, dog shows and other places where dogs congregate to try to minimize spread of infection.

Leptospirosis: A potentially fatal disease that is more common in some geographic regions. It is capable of being spread to humans. The disease varies with the individual "serovar," or strain, of *Leptospira* involved. Since there does not appear to be much cross-protection between serovars, protection is only as good as the likelihood that the serovar in the vaccine is the same as the one in the pet's local environment. Problems with *Leptospira* vaccines are that protection does not last very long, side effects are not uncommon and a large percentage of dogs (perhaps 30%) may not respond to vaccination.

Borrelia burgdorferi: The cause of Lyme disease, the risk of which varies with the geographic area in which the pet lives and travels. Lyme disease is spread by deer ticks in the eastern US and western black-legged ticks in the western part of the country, and the risk of exposure is high in some regions. Lameness, fever and inappetence are most commonly seen in affected dogs. The extent of protection from the vaccine has not been conclusively demonstrated.

Coronavirus: This disease has a high risk of exposure, especially in areas where dogs congregate, but it typically causes only mild to moderate digestive upset (diarrhea, vomiting, etc.). Vaccines are available, but the duration of protection is believed to be relatively short and the effectiveness of the vaccine in preventing infection is considered low.

There are many other vaccinations available, including those for *Giardia* and canine adenovirus-1. While there may be some specific indications for their use, and local risk factors to be considered, they are not widely recommended for most dogs.

FOOD ALLERGY

Severe itching, leading to bald patches and open sores on the feet, face, ears, armpits and groin, could be caused by a food allergy. Studies indicate that up to 10% of dogs suffer from food allergies, which develop slowly over time without a change in diet. Dogs who suffer from chronic ear problems may actually have a food allergy. Unfortunately, there are no tests available to determine whether your dog definitely suffers from a food allergy. The dog will be miserable and you will be frustrated and stressed.

Take the problem into your own hands and kitchen. Select a type of meat that your dog is not getting from his existing diet, perhaps white fish, lamb or venison, and prepare a home-cooked food. The food should consist of two parts carbohydrate (rice, pasta or potatoes) and one part protein (the chosen meat). It's better not to start with soy as the protein source unless all of the meats cause a reaction.

Monitor your dog's intake carefully. He must eat only your prepared meal without any treats or side-trips to the garbage can. All family members (and visiting friends) must be informed of the plan. After four or five weeks on the new diet, you will reintroduce a portion of his original diet to determine whether this food is the cause of the allergic reaction. Once the dog reacts to the change in diet, resume the new diet. Make dietary modifications every two weeks and keep careful records of any reactions.

necessary to reevaluate the situation and deal with some tough questions. It is important to realize that whether or not to use a particular vaccine depends on the risk of contracting the disease against which it protects, the severity of the disease if it is contracted, the duration of immunity provided by the vaccine, the safety of the product and the needs of the individual animal. In a very general sense, rabies, distemper, hepatitis and parvovirus are considered core vaccine needs, while parainfluenza, *Bordetella bronchiseptica*, leptospirosis, coronavirus and borreliosis (Lyme disease) are considered non-core needs and best reserved for animals that demonstrate reasonable risk of contracting the diseases.

As soft and inviting as the grass may be, fleas, ticks and other pests frequently infest these areas, waiting for an unsuspecting target. Parasite problems and insect bites are common afflictions during the summer months.

NEUTERING/SPAYING

Sterilization procedures (neutering for males/spaying for females) are meant to accomplish several purposes. While the underlying

When grooming your Whippet, be on guard for abnormalities of the skin and coat.

premise is to address the risk of pet overpopulation, there are also some medical and behavioral benefits to the surgeries as well. For females, spaying prior to the first estrus (heat cycle) leads to a marked reduction in the risk of mammary cancer. There also will be no manifestations of "heat" to attract male dogs and no bleeding in the house. For males, there is prevention of testicular cancer and a reduction in the risk of prostate problems. In both sexes there may be some limited reduction in aggressive behaviors toward other dogs, and some diminishing of urine marking, roaming and mounting.

While neutering and spaying do indeed prevent animals from contributing to pet overpopulation, even no-cost and low-cost neutering options have not eliminated the problem. Perhaps one of the main reasons for this is that

individuals who intentionally breed their dogs and those who allow their animals to run at large are the main causes of unwanted offspring. Also, animals in shelters are often there because they were abandoned or relinquished, not because they came from unplanned matings. Neutering/ spaying is important, but it should be considered in the context of the real causes of animals' ending up in shelters and eventually being euthanized.

One of the important considerations regarding neutering is that it is a surgical procedure. This sometimes gets lost in discussions of low-cost procedures and commoditization of the process. In females, spaying is specifically referred to as an ovariohysterectomy. In this procedure, a midline incision is made in the abdomen, and the entire uterus and both ovaries are surgically removed. While this is a major invasive surgical procedure,

HEARTWORM ZONE

Although heartworm cases have been reported in all 48 continental states, the largest threat exists in the Southeast and Mississippi River Valley. The following states have the highest risk factors: Texas, Florida, Louisiana, North Carolina, Georgia, Mississippi, Tennessee, South Carolina, Alabama and Indiana. Discuss the risk factor with your veterinarian to determine the safest course of prevention for your dog.

it usually has few complications because it is typically performed on healthy young animals. However, it is major surgery, as any woman who has had a hysterectomy will attest.

In males, neutering has traditionally referred to castration, which involves the surgical removal of both testicles. While still a significant piece of surgery, there is not the abdominal exposure that is required in the female surgery. In addition, there is now a chemical sterilization option, in which a solution is injected into each testicle, leading to atrophy of the sperm-producing cells. This can typically be done under sedation rather than full anesthesia. This is a relatively new approach, and there are no long-term clinical studies yet available.

Neutering/spaying is typically done around six months of age at most veterinary hospitals, although techniques have been pioneered to perform the procedures in animals as young as eight weeks of age. In general, the surgeries on the very young animals are done for the specific reason of sterilizing them before they go to their new homes. This is done in some shelter hospitals for assurance that the animals will definitely not produce any pups. Otherwise, these organizations need to rely on owners to comply with their wishes to have the animals "altered" at a later date, something that does not always happen.

There are some exciting immunocontraceptive "vaccines" currently under development, and there may be a time when contraception in pets will not require surgical procedures. We anxiously await these developments.

DOGGIE DENTAL DON'TS

A veterinary dental exam is necessary if you notice one or any combination of the following in your dog:

- Broken, loose or missing teeth
- Loss of appetite (which could be due to mouth pain or illness caused by infection)
- Gum abnormalities, including redness, swelling and bleeding
- Drooling, with or without blood
- Yellowing of the teeth or gumline, indicating tartar
- Bad breath

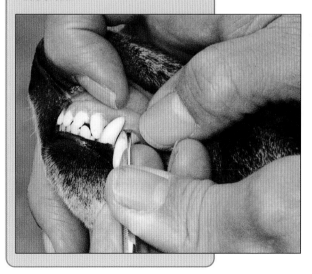

S. E. M. BY DR. DENNIS KUNKEL, UNIVERSITY OF HAWAII.

A scanning electron micrograph of a dog flea, Ctenocephalides canis, on dog hair.

EXTERNAL PARASITES

FLEAS

Fleas have been around for millions of years and, while we have better tools now for controlling them than at any time in the past, there still is little chance that they will end up on an endangered species list. Actually, they are very well adapted to living on our pets, and they continue to adapt as we make advances.

The female flea can consume 15 times her weight in blood during active reproduction and can lay as many as 40 eggs a day. These eggs are very resistant to the effects of insecticides. They hatch into larvae, which then mature and spin cocoons. The immature fleas reside in this pupal stage until the time is right for feeding. This pupal stage is also very resistant to the effects of insecticides, and pupae can last in the environment without feeding for many months. Newly emergent fleas are attracted to animals by the warmth of the animals' bodies, movement and exhaled carbon dioxide. However, when they first emerge from their cocoons, they orient towards light; thus, when an animal passes between a flea and the light source, casting a shadow, the flea pounces and starts to feed. If the animal turns out to be a dog or cat, the reproductive cycle continues. If the flea lands on another type of animal, including a person, the flea will bite but will then look for a more appropriate host. An emerging adult flea can survive without feeding for up to 12 months but, once it tastes blood, it can survive off its host for only three to four days.

It was once thought that fleas spend most of their lives in the environment, but we now know that fleas won't willingly jump off a dog unless leaping to another dog or when physically removed by brushing, bathing or other manipulation. Flea eggs, on the other hand, are shiny and smooth, and they roll off the animal and into the environment. The eggs, larvae and pupae then exist in the environment, but once the adult finds a susceptible animal, it's home sweet home until the flea is forced to seek refuge elsewhere.

Since adult fleas live on the animal and immature forms survive in the environment, a successful treatment plan must address all stages of the flea life cycle. There are now several safe and effective flea-control products that can be applied on a monthly basis. These include

FLEA PREVENTION FOR YOUR DOG

- Discuss with your veterinarian the safest product to protect your dog, likely in the form of a monthly tablet or a liquid preparation placed on the back of the dog's neck.
- For dogs suffering from flea-bite dermatitis, a shampoo or topical insecticide treatment is required.
- Your lawn and property should be sprayed with an insecticide designed to kill fleas and ticks that lurk outdoors.
- Using a flea comb, check the dog's coat regularly for any signs of parasites.
- Practice good housekeeping. Vacuum floors, carpets and furniture regularly, especially in the areas that the dog frequents, and wash the dog's bedding weekly.
- Follow up house-cleaning with carpet shampoos and sprays to rid the house of fleas at all stages of development. Insect growth regulators are the safest option.

fipronil, imidacloprid, selamectin and permethrin (found in several formulations). Most of these products have significant flea-killing rates within 24 hours. However, none of them will control the immature forms in the environment. To accomplish this, there are a variety of insect growth regulators that can be sprayed into the

THE FLEA'S LIFE CYCLE

What came first, the flea or the egg? This age-old mystery is more difficult to comprehend than the

actual cycle of the flea. Fleas usually live only about four months. A female can lay 2,000 eggs in her lifetime.

Egg

After ten days of rolling around your carpet or under your furniture, the eggs hatch into larvae,

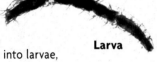

Larva

which feed on various and sundry debris. In days or months, depending on the climate, the larvae spin cocoons and develop into the pupal or nymph stage, which quickly develop into fleas.

Pupa

These immature fleas must locate a host within 10 to 14 days or they will die. Only about 1% of the flea population exist as adult fleas, while the other 99% exist as eggs, larvae or pupae.

KILL FLEAS THE NATURAL WAY

If you choose not to go the route of conventional medication, there are some natural ways to ward off fleas:

- Dust your dog with a natural flea powder, composed of such herbal goodies as rosemary, wormwood, pennyroyal, citronella, rue, tobacco powder and eucalyptus.
- Apply diatomaceous earth, the fossilized remains of single-cell algae, to your carpets, furniture and pet's bedding. Even though it's not good for dogs, it's even worse for fleas, which will dry up swiftly and die.
- Brush your dog frequently, give him adequate exercise and let him fast occasionally. All of these activities strengthen the dog's system and make him more resistant to disease and parasites.
- Bathe your dog with a capful of pennyroyal or eucalyptus oil.
- Feed a natural diet, free of additives and preservatives. Add some fresh garlic and brewer's yeast to the dog's morning portion, as these items have flea-repelling properties.

environment (e.g., pyriproxyfen, methoprene, fenoxycarb) as well as insect development inhibitors such as lufenuron that can be administered. These compounds have no effect on adult fleas, but they stop immature forms from developing into adults. In years gone by we relied heavily on toxic insecticides (such as organophosphates, organochlorines and carbamates) to manage the flea problem, but today's options are not only much safer to use on our pets but also safer for the environment.

TICKS

Ticks are members of the spider class (arachnids) and are blood-sucking parasites capable of transmitting a variety of diseases, including Lyme disease, ehrlichiosis, babesiosis and Rocky Mountain spotted fever. It's easy to see ticks on your own skin, but it is more of a challenge when your furry companion is affected. Whenever you happen to be planning a stroll in a tick-infested area (especially forests, grassy or wooded areas or parks) be prepared to do a thorough inspection of your dog afterward to search for ticks. Ticks can be tricky, so make sure you spend time looking in the ears, between the toes and everywhere else where a tick might hide. Ticks need to be attached for 24–72 hours before they transmit most of the diseases that they carry, so you do have a window of opportunity for some preventive intervention.

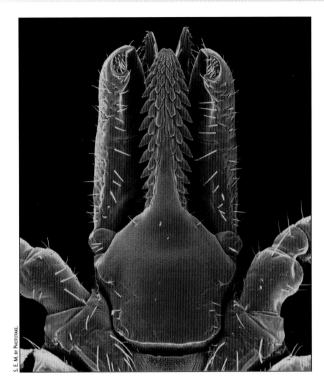

S. E. M. BY PHOTOTAKE.

A TICKING BOMB

There is nothing good about a tick's harpooning his nose into your dog's skin. Among the diseases caused by ticks are Rocky Mountain spotted fever, canine ehrlichiosis, canine babesiosis, canine hepatozoonosis and Lyme disease. If a dog is allergic to the saliva of a female wood tick, he can develop tick paralysis.

Female ticks live to eat and breed. They can lay between 4,000 and 5,000 eggs and they die soon after. Males, on the other hand, live only to mate with the females and continue the process as long as they are able. Most ticks live on multiple hosts before parasitizing dogs. The immature forms typically reside on grass and shrubs, waiting for susceptible animals to walk by. The larvae and nymph stages typically feed on wildlife.

If only a few ticks are present on a dog, they can be plucked out, but it is important to remove the entire head and mouthparts,

A scanning electron micrograph of the head of a female deer tick, *Ixodes dammini*, a parasitic tick that carries Lyme disease.

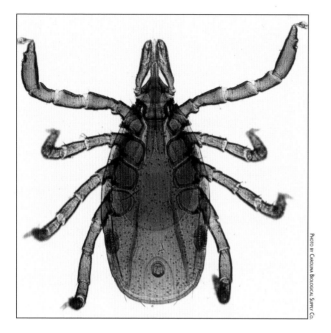

Deer tick, *Ixodes dammini.*

Photo by Carolina Biological Supply Co.

gion. The tick should be disposed of in a container of alcohol or household bleach.

Some of the newer flea products, specifically those with fipronil, selamectin and permethrin, have effect against some, but not all, species of tick. Flea collars containing appropriate pesticides (e.g., propoxur, chlorfenvinphos) can aid in tick control. In most areas, such collars should be placed on animals in March, at the beginning of the tick season, and changed regularly. Leaving the collar on when the pesticide level is waning invites the development of resistance. Amitraz collars are also good for tick control, and the active ingredient does not interfere with other flea-control products. The ingredient helps prevent the attachment of ticks to the skin and will cause those ticks already on the skin to detach themselves.

which may be deeply embedded in the skin. This is best accomplished with forceps designed especially for this purpose; fingers can be used but should be protected with rubber gloves, plastic wrap or at least a paper towel. The tick should be grasped as closely as possible to the animal's skin and should be pulled upward with steady, even pressure. Do not squeeze, crush or puncture the body of the tick or you risk exposure to any disease carried by that tick. Once the ticks have been removed, the sites of attachment should be disinfected. Your hands should then be washed with soap and water to further minimize risk of conta-

TICK CONTROL

Removal of underbrush and leaf litter and the thinning of trees in areas where tick control is desired are recommended. These actions remove the cover and food sources for small animals that serve as hosts for ticks. With continued mowing of grasses in these areas, the probability of ticks' surviving is further reduced. A variety of insecticide ingredients (e.g., resmethrin, carbaryl, permethrin, chlorpyrifos, dioxathion and allethrin) are registered for tick control around the home.

MITES

Mites are tiny arachnid parasites that parasitize the skin of dogs. Skin diseases caused by mites are referred to as "mange," and there are many different forms seen in dogs. These forms are very different from one another, each one warranting an individual description.

Sarcoptic mange, or scabies, is one of the itchiest conditions that affects dogs. The microscopic *Sarcoptes* mites burrow into the superficial layers of the skin and can drive dogs crazy with itchiness. They are also communicable to people, although they can't complete their reproductive cycle on people. In addition to being tiny, the mites also are often difficult to find when trying to make a diagnosis. Skin scrapings from multiple areas are examined microscopically but, even then, sometimes the mites cannot be found.

Fortunately, scabies is relatively easy to treat, and there are a variety of products that will successfully kill the mites. Since the mites can't live in the environment for very long without feeding, a complete cure is usually possible within four to eight weeks.

Cheyletiellosis is caused by a relatively large mite, which sometimes can be seen even without a microscope. Often referred to as "walking dandruff," this also causes itching, but not usually as profound as with scabies. While *Cheyletiella* mites can survive

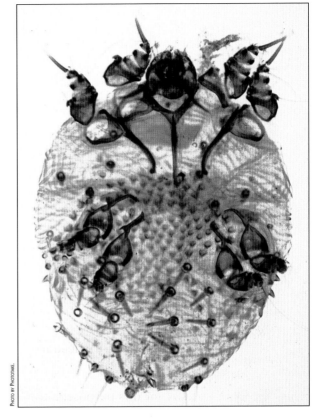

PHOTO BY PHOTOTAKE.

Sarcoptes scabiei, commonly known as the "itch mite."

somewhat longer in the environment than scabies mites, they too are relatively easy to treat, being responsive to not only the medications used to treat scabies but also often to flea-control products.

Otodectes cynotis is the canine ear mite and is one of the more common causes of mange, especially in young dogs in shelters or pet stores. That's because the mites are typically present in large numbers and are quickly spread to nearby animals. The mites rarely do much harm but

Micrograph of a dog louse, *Heterodoxus spiniger*. Female lice attach their eggs to the hairs of the dog. As the eggs hatch, the larval lice bite and feed on the blood. Lice can also feed on dead skin and hair. This feeding activity can cause hair loss and skin problems.

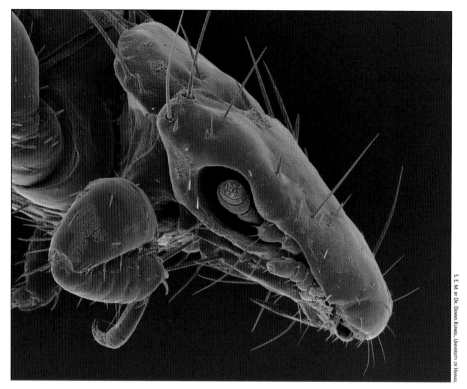

S. E. M. by Dr. Dennis Kunkel, University of Hawaii.

can be difficult to eradicate if the treatment regimen is not comprehensive. While many try to treat the condition with ear drops only, this is the most common cause of treatment failure. Ear drops cause the mites to simply move out of the ears and as far away as possible (usually to the base of the tail) until the insecticide levels in the ears drop to an acceptable level— then it's back to business as usual! The successful treatment of ear mites requires treating all animals in the household with a systemic insecticide, such as selamectin, or a combination of miticidal ear drops combined with whole-body flea-control preparations.

Demodicosis, sometimes referred to as red mange, can be one of the most difficult forms of mange to treat. Part of the problem has to do with the fact that the mites live in the hair follicles and they are relatively well shielded from topical and systemic products. The main issue, however, is that demodectic mange typically results only when there is some underlying process interfering with the dog's immune system.

Since *Demodex* mites are normal residents of the skin of

mammals, including humans, there is usually a mite population explosion only when the immune system fails to keep the number of mites in check. In young animals, the immune deficit may be transient or may reflect an actual inherited immune problem. In older animals, demodicosis is usually seen only when there is another disease hampering the immune system, such as diabetes, cancer, thyroid problems or the use of immune-suppressing drugs. Accordingly, treatment involves not only trying to kill the mange mites but also discerning what is interfering with immune function and correcting it if possible.

Chiggers represent several different species of mite that don't parasitize dogs specifically, but do latch on to passersby and can cause irritation. The problem is most prevalent in wooded areas in the late summer and fall. Treatment is not difficult, as the mites do not complete their life cycle on dogs and are susceptible to a variety of miticidal products.

MOSQUITOES

Mosquitoes have long been known to transmit a variety of diseases to people, as well as just being biting pests during warm weather. They also pose a real risk to pets. Not only do they carry deadly heartworms but

recently there also has been much concern over their involvement with West Nile virus. While we can avoid heartworm with the use of preventive medications, there are no such preventives for West Nile virus. The only method of prevention in endemic areas is active mosquito control. Fortunately, most dogs that have been exposed to the virus only developed flu-like symptoms and, to date, there have not been the large number of reported deaths in canines as seen in some other species.

Illustration of
*Demodex
folliculoram.*

MOSQUITO REPELLENT

Low concentrations of DEET (less than 10%), found in many human mosquito repellents, have been safely used in dogs but, in these concentrations, probably give only about two hours of protection. DEET may be safe in these small concentrations, but since it is not licensed for use on dogs, there is no research proving its safety for dogs. Products containing permethrin give the longest-lasting protection, perhaps two to four weeks. As DEET is not licensed for use on dogs, and both DEET and permethrin can be quite toxic to cats, appropriate care should be exercised. Other products, such as those containing oil of citronella, also have some mosquito-repellent activity, but typically have a relatively short duration of action.

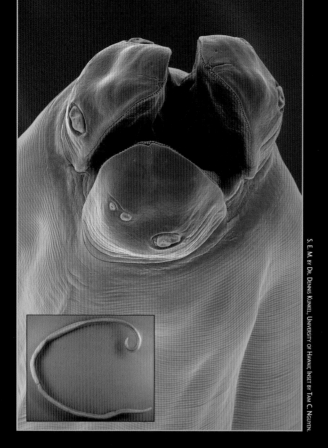

The vertical text along the image reads: S. E. M. BY DR. DENNIS KUNKEL, UNIVERSITY OF HAWAII; INSET BY TAM C. NGUYEN.

The ascarid roundworm *Toxocara canis*, showing the mouth with three lips. INSET: Photomicrograph of the round-worm *Ascaris lumbricoides*.

INTERNAL PARASITES: WORMS

ASCARIDS

Ascarids are intestinal round-worms that rarely cause severe disease in dogs. Nonetheless, they are of major public health signifi-cance because they can be trans-ferred to people. Sadly, it is chil-dren who are most commonly affected by the parasite, probably from inadvertently ingesting ascarid-contaminated soil. In fact, many yards and children's sand-boxes contain appreciable numbers of ascarid eggs. So, while ascarids don't bite dogs or latch onto their intestines to suck blood, they do cause some nasty medical conditions in children and are best eradicated from our furry friends. Because pups can start passing ascarid eggs by three weeks of age, most parasite-control programs begin at two weeks of age and are repeated every two weeks until pups are eight weeks old. It is important to

HOOKED ON ANCYLOSTOMA

Adult dogs can become infected by the bloodsucking nematodes we commonly call hookworms via ingesting larvae from the ground or via the larvae penetrating the dog's skin. It is not uncommon for infected dogs to show no symptoms of hookworm infestation. Sometimes symptoms occur within ten days of exposure. These symptoms can include bloody diarrhea, anemia, loss of weight and general weakness. Dogs pass the hookworm eggs in their stools, which serves as the vet's method of identifying the infestation. The hookworm larvae can encyst themselves in the dog's tissues and be released when the dog is experiencing stress.

Caused by an *Ancylostoma* species whose common host is the dog, cutaneous larval migrans affects humans, causing itching and lumps and streaks beneath the surface of the skin.

S. E. M. BY DR. DENNIS KUNKEL, UNIVERSITY OF HAWAII.

realize that bitches can pass ascarids to their pups even if they test negative prior to whelping. Accordingly, bitches are best treated at the same time as the pups.

HOOKWORMS

Unlike ascarids, hookworms do latch onto a dog's intestinal tract and can cause significant loss of blood and protein. Similar to ascarids, hookworms can be transmitted to humans, where they cause a condition known as cutaneous larval migrans. Dogs can become infected either by consuming the infective larvae or by the larvae's penetrating the skin directly. People most often get infected when they are lying on the ground (such as on a beach) and the larvae penetrate the skin. Yes, the larvae can penetrate through a beach blanket. Hookworms are typically susceptible to the same medications used to treat ascarids.

The hookworm *Ancylostoma caninum* infests the intestines of dogs. INSET: Note the row of hooks at the posterior end, used to anchor the worm to the intestinal wall.

WHIPWORMS

Whipworms latch onto the lower aspects of the dog's colon and can cause cramping and diarrhea. Eggs do not start to appear in the dog's feces until about three months after the dog was infected. This worm has a peculiar life cycle, which makes it more difficult to control than ascarids or hookworms. The good thing is that whipworms rarely are transferred to people.

Some of the medications used to treat ascarids and hookworms are also effective against whipworms, but, in general, a separate treatment protocol is needed. Since most of the medications are effective against the adults but not the eggs or larvae, treatment is typically repeated in three weeks, and then

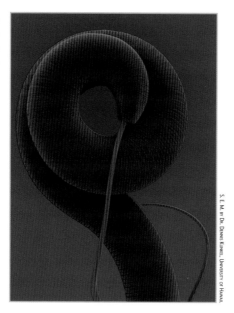

Adult whipworm, *Trichuris* sp., an intestinal parasite.

S. E. M. BY DR. DENNIS KUNKEL, UNIVERSITY OF HAWAII.

WORM-CONTROL GUIDELINES

- Practice sanitary habits with your dog and home.
- Clean up after your dog and don't let him sniff or eat other dogs' droppings.
- Control insects and fleas in the dog's environment. Fleas, lice, cockroaches, beetles, mice and rats can act as hosts for various worms.
- Prevent dogs from eating uncooked meat, raw poultry and dead animals.
- Keep dogs and children from playing in sand and soil.
- Kennel dogs on cement or gravel; avoid dirt runs.
- Administer heartworm preventives regularly.
- Have your vet examine your dog's stools at your annual visits.
- Select a boarding kennel carefully so as to avoid contamination from other dogs or an unsanitary environment.
- Prevent dogs from roaming. Obey local leash laws.

---

often in three months as well. Unfortunately, since dogs don't develop resistance to whipworms, it is difficult to prevent them from getting reinfected if they visit soil contaminated with whipworm eggs.

TAPEWORMS

There are many different species of tapeworm that affect dogs, but *Dipylidium caninum* is probably the most common and is spread by fleas. Flea larvae feed on organic debris and tapeworm eggs in the environment and, when a dog chews at himself and manages to ingest fleas, he might get a dose of tapeworm at the same time. The tapeworm then develops further in the intestine of the dog.

The tapeworm itself, which is a flatworm that latches onto the intestinal wall, is composed of numerous segments. When the segments break off into the intestine (as proglottids), they may accumulate around the rectum, like grains of rice. While this tapeworm is disgusting in its behavior, it is not directly communicable to humans (although humans can also get infected by swallowing fleas).

A much more dangerous flatworm is *Echinococcus multilocularis*, which is typically found in foxes, coyotes and wolves. The eggs are passed in the feces and infect rodents, and, when dogs eat the rodents, the dogs can be infected by thousands of adult tapeworms. While the parasites don't cause many problems in dogs, this is considered the most lethal worm infection that people can get. Take appropriate precautions if you live in an area in which these tapeworms are found. Do not use mulch that may contain feces of dogs, cats or wildlife, and discourage your pets from hunting

wildlife. Treat these tapeworm infections aggressively in pets, because if humans get infected, approximately half die.

HEARTWORMS

Heartworm disease is caused by the parasite *Dirofilaria immitis* and is seen in dogs around the world. A member of the roundworm group, it is spread between dogs by the bite of an infected mosquito. The mosquito injects infective larvae into the dog's skin with its bite, and these larvae develop under the skin for a period of time before making their way to the heart. There they develop into adults, which grow and create blockages of the heart, lungs and major blood vessels there. They also start producing offspring (microfilariae)

A dog tapeworm proglottid (body segment).

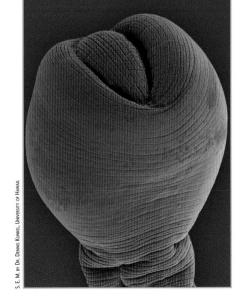

The dog tapeworm *Taenia pisiformis*.

A Look at Internal Parasites

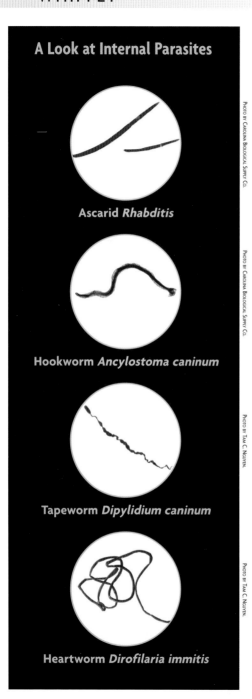

Ascarid *Rhabditis*

Hookworm *Ancylostoma caninum*

Tapeworm *Dipylidium caninum*

Heartworm *Dirofilaria immitis*

and these microfilariae circulate in the bloodstream, waiting to hitch a ride when the next mosquito bites. Once in the mosquito, the microfilariae develop into infective larvae and the entire process is repeated.

When dogs get infected with heartworm, over time they tend to develop symptoms associated with heart disease, such as coughing, exercise intolerance and potentially many other manifestations. Diagnosis is confirmed by either seeing the microfilariae themselves in blood samples or using immunologic tests (antigen testing) to identify the presence of adult heartworms. Since antigen tests measure the presence of adult heartworms and microfilarial tests measure offspring produced by adults, neither are positive until six to seven months after the initial infection. However, the beginning of damage can occur by fifth-stage larvae as early as three months after infection. Thus it is possible for dogs to be harboring problem-causing larvae for up to three months before either type of test would identify an infection.

The good news is that there are great protocols available for preventing heartworm in dogs. Testing is critical in the process, and it is important to understand the benefits as well as the limitations of such testing. All dogs six months of age or older that have not been on continuous heartworm-preventive

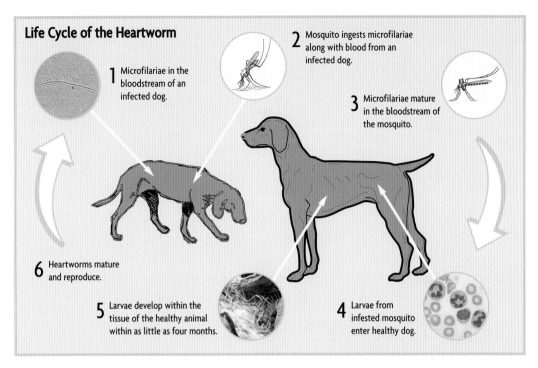

Life Cycle of the Heartworm

1 Microfilariae in the bloodstream of an infected dog.

2 Mosquito ingests microfilariae along with blood from an infected dog.

3 Microfilariae mature in the bloodstream of the mosquito.

6 Heartworms mature and reproduce.

5 Larvae develop within the tissue of the healthy animal within as little as four months.

4 Larvae from infested mosquito enter healthy dog.

medication should be screened with microfilarial or antigen tests. For dogs receiving preventive medication, periodic antigen testing helps assess the effectiveness of the preventives. The American Heart-worm Society guidelines suggest that annual retesting may not be necessary when owners have absolutely provided continuous heartworm prevention. Retesting on a two- to three-year interval may be sufficient in these cases. However, your veterinarian will likely have specific guidelines under which heartworm preventives will be prescribed, and many prefer to err on the side of safety and retest annually.

It is indeed fortunate that heartworm is relatively easy to prevent, because treatments can be as life-threatening as the disease itself. Treatment requires a two-step process that kills the adult heartworms first and then the microfilariae. Prevention is obviously preferable; this involves a once-monthly oral or topical treatment. The most common oral preventives include ivermectin (not suitable for some breeds), moxidectin and milbe-mycin oxime; the once-a-month topical drug selamectin provides heartworm protection in addition to flea, tick and other parasite controls.

THE **ABC**S OF
Emergency Care

Abrasions
Clean wound with running water or 3% hydrogen peroxide. Pat dry with gauze and spray with antibiotic. Do not cover.

Animal Bites
Clean area with soap and saline solution or water. Apply pressure to any bleeding area. Apply antibiotic ointment.

Antifreeze Poisoning
Induce vomiting and take dog to the vet.

Bee Sting
Remove stinger and apply soothing lotion or cold compress; give antihistamine in proper dosage.

Bleeding
Apply pressure directly to wound with gauze or towel for five to ten minutes. If wound does not stop bleeding, wrap wound with gauze and adhesive tape.

Bloat/Gastric Torsion
Immediately take the dog to the vet or emergency clinic; phone from car. No time to waste.

Burns
Chemical: Bathe dog with water and pet shampoo. Rinse in saline solution. Apply antibiotic ointment.

Acid: Rinse with water. Apply one part baking soda, two parts water to affected area.

Alkali: Rinse with water. Apply one part vinegar, four parts water to affected area.

Electrical: Apply antibiotic ointment. Seek veterinary assistance immediately.

Choking
If the dog is on the verge of collapsing, wedge a solid object, such as the handle of screwdriver, between molars on one side of the mouth to keep mouth open. Pull tongue out. Use long-nosed pliers or fingers to remove foreign object. Do not push the object down the dog's throat. For small or medium dogs, hold dog upside down by hind legs and shake firmly to dislodge foreign object.

Chlorine Ingestion
With clean water, rinse the mouth and eyes. Give the dog water to drink; contact the vet.

Constipation
Feed dog 2 tablespoons bran flakes with each meal. Encourage drinking water. Mix 1/4 teaspoon mineral oil in dog's food.

Diarrhea
Withhold food for 12 to 24 hours. Feed dog anti-diarrheal with eyedropper. When feeding resumes, feed one part boiled hamburger, one part plain cooked rice, 1/4 to 3/4 cup four times daily.

Dog Bite
Snip away hair around puncture wound; clean with 3% hydrogen peroxide; apply tincture of iodine. If wound appears deep, take the dog to the vet.

Frostbite
Wrap the dog in a heavy blanket. Warm affected area with a warm bath for ten minutes. Red color to skin will return with circulation; if tissues are pale after 20 minutes, contact the vet.

Use a portable, durable container large enough to contain all items

Heat Stroke
Submerge the dog in cold water; if no response within ten minutes, contact the vet.

Hot Spots
Mix 2 packets Domeboro® with 2 cups water. Saturate cloth with mixture and apply to hot spots for 15-30 minutes. Apply antibiotic ointment. Repeat every six to eight hours.

Poisonous Plants
Wash affected area with soap and water. Cleanse with alcohol. For foxtail/grass, apply antibiotic ointment.

Rat Poison Ingestion
Induce vomiting. Keep dog calm, maintain dog's normal body temperature (use blanket or heating pad). Get to the vet for antidote.

Shock
Keep the dog calm and warm; call for veterinary assistance.

Snake Bite
If possible, bandage the area and apply pressure. If the area is not conducive to bandaging, use ice to control bleeding. Get immediate help from the vet.

Tick Removal
Apply flea and tick spray directly on tick. Wait one minute. Using tweezers or wearing plastic gloves, grasp the tick's body firmly. Apply antibiotic ointment.

Vomiting
Restrict dog's water intake; offer a few ice cubes. Withhold food for next meal. Contact vet if vomiting persists longer than 24 hours.

DOG OWNER'S FIRST-AID KIT
- ❏ **Gauze bandages/swabs**
- ❏ **Adhesive and non-adhesive bandages**
- ❏ **Antibiotic powder**
- ❏ **Antiseptic wash**
- ❏ **Hydrogen peroxide 3%**
- ❏ **Antibiotic ointment**
- ❏ **Lubricating jelly**
- ❏ **Rectal thermometer**
- ❏ **Nylon muzzle**
- ❏ **Scissors and forceps**
- ❏ **Eyedropper**
- ❏ **Syringe**
- ❏ **Anti-bacterial/fungal solution**
- ❏ **Saline solution**
- ❏ **Antihistamine**
- ❏ **Cotton balls**
- ❏ **Nail clippers**
- ❏ **Screwdriver/pen knife**
- ❏ **Flashlight**
- ❏ **Emergency phone numbers**

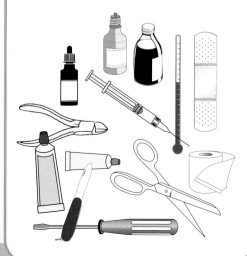

WHIPPET

When we bring home a puppy, we hope for a long, happy and fulfilling relationship with the new family member. Even when we adopt an older dog, we look forward to the years of companionship ahead with a new canine friend. However, aging is inevitable for all creatures.

In general, purebred dogs are considered to have achieved senior status when they reach 75% of their breed's average lifespan, with lifespan being based on breed size and breed-specific

factors. Your Whippet has an average lifespan of 14, which is a long life for any breed, and thus is a senior citizen at around 10 years old.

Obviously, the old "seven dog years to one human year" theory is not exact. In puppyhood, a dog's year is actually comparable to more than seven human years, considering the puppy's rapid growth during his first year. Then, in adulthood, the ratio decreases. The more viable rule of thumb is that the larger the dog, the shorter his expected lifespan. Of course, this can vary among individuals, with many living longer than expected, which we hope!

WHAT ARE THE SIGNS?
By the time your dog has reached his senior years, you will know him very well, so the physical and behavioral changes that accompany aging should be noticeable to you. Humans and dogs share the most obvious physical sign of aging: gray hair! Graying often occurs first on the muzzle and face, around the eyes. Other telltale signs are the dog's

Many Whippets remain sprightly and active into their senior years, but they then will need more frequent periods of rest.

overall decrease in activity. Your older dog might be more content to nap and rest, and he may not show the same old enthusiasm when it's time to play in the yard or go for a walk. Other physical signs include significant weight loss or gain; more labored movement; skin and coat problems, possibly hair loss; sight and/or hearing problems; changes in toileting habits, perhaps seeming "unhousebroken" at times; tooth decay, bad breath or other mouth problems.

There are behavioral changes that go along with aging, too. There are numerous causes for behavioral changes. Sometimes a dog's apparent confusion results from a physical change like diminished sight or hearing. If his confusion causes him to be afraid, he may act aggressively or defensively. He may sleep more frequently because his daily

---

WHAT A RELIEF!

Much like young puppies, older dogs do not have as much control over their excretory functions as they do as non-seniors. Their muscle control fades and, as such, they cannot "hold it" for as long as they used to. This is easily remedied by additional trips outside. If your dog's sight is failing, have the yard well lit at night and/or lead him to his relief site on lead. Incontinence should be discussed with your vet.

---

walks, though shorter now, tire him out. He may begin to experience separation anxiety or, conversely, become less interested in petting and attention.

There also are clinical conditions that cause behavioral changes in older dogs. One such condition is known as cognitive dysfunction (familiarly known as "old-dog" syndrome). It can be frustrating for an owner whose dog is affected with cognitive dysfunction, as it can result in behavioral changes of all types, most seemingly unexplainable. Common changes include the dog's forgetting aspects of the daily routine, such as times to eat, go out for walks, relieve himself and the like. Along the same lines, you may take your dog out at the regular time for a potty trip and he may have no idea why he is there. Sometimes a placid dog will begin to show aggressive or possessive tendencies or, conversely, a hyperactive dog will start to "mellow out."

Disease also can be the cause of behavioral changes in senior dogs. Hormonal problems (Cushing's disease is common in older dogs), diabetes and thyroid disease can cause increased appetite, which can lead to aggression related to food guarding. It's better to be proactive with your senior dog, making more frequent trips to the vet if necessary and having bloodwork done

Number-One Killer Disease in Dogs: CANCER

In every age, there is a word associated with a disease or plague that causes humans to shudder. In the 21st century, that word is "cancer." Just as cancer is the leading cause of death in humans, it claims nearly half the lives of dogs that die from a natural disease as well as half the dogs that die over the age of ten years.

Described as a genetic disease, cancer becomes a greater risk as the dog ages. Vets and dog owners have become increasingly aware of the threat of cancer to dogs. Statistics reveal that one dog in every five will develop cancer, the most common of which is skin cancer. Many cancers, including prostate, ovarian and breast cancer, can be avoided by spaying and neutering our dogs by the age of six months.

Early detection of cancer can save or extend a dog's life, so it is absolutely vital for owners to have their dogs examined by a qualified vet or oncologist immediately upon detection of any abnormality. Certain dietary guidelines have also proven to reduce the onset and spread of cancer. Foods based on fish rather than beef, due to the presence of Omega-3 fatty acids, are recommended. Other amino acids such as glutamine have significant benefits for canines, particularly those breeds that show a greater susceptibility to cancer.

Cancer management and treatments promise hope for future generations of canines. Since the disease is genetic, breeders should never breed a dog whose parents, grandparents and any related siblings have developed cancer. It is difficult to know whether to exclude an otherwise healthy dog from a breeding program, as the disease does not manifest itself until the dog's senior years.

RECOGNIZE CANCER WARNING SIGNS

Since early detection can possibly rescue your dog from becoming a cancer statistic, it is essential for owners to recognize the possible signs and seek the assistance of a qualified professional.

- Abnormal bumps or lumps that continue to grow
- Bleeding or discharge from any body cavity
- Persistent stiffness or lameness
- Recurrent sores or sores that do not heal
- Inappetence
- Breathing difficulties
- Weight loss
- Bad breath or odors
- General malaise and fatigue
- Eating and swallowing problems
- Difficulty urinating and defecating

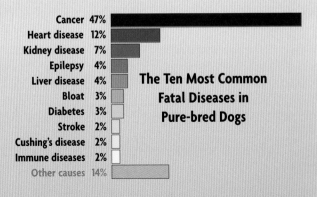

Cancer	47%
Heart disease	12%
Kidney disease	7%
Epilepsy	4%
Liver disease	4%
Bloat	3%
Diabetes	3%
Stroke	2%
Cushing's disease	2%
Immune diseases	2%
Other causes	14%

The Ten Most Common Fatal Diseases in Pure-bred Dogs

to test for the diseases that can commonly befall older dogs.

The aforementioned changes are discussed to alert owners to the things that may happen as their dogs get older. Many hardy dogs remain active and alert well into old age. However, it can be frustrating and heartbreaking for owners to see their beloved dogs change physically and temperamentally. Just know that it's the same Whippet under there, and that he still loves you and appreciates your care, which he needs now more than ever.

CARING FOR MY AGING DOG

Your dog might reach the estimated "senior" age for Whippets and show no signs of slowing down. However, even if he shows no outward signs of aging, he should begin a senior-care program once he reaches the determined age. By providing him with extra attention to his veterinary care at this age, you will be practicing good preventive medicine, ensuring that the rest of your dog's life will be as long, active, happy and healthy as possible. If you do notice indications of aging, such as graying and/or changes in sleeping, eating or toileting habits, this is a sign to set up a senior-care visit with your vet right away to make sure that these changes are not related to any health problems.

To start, senior dogs should visit the vet twice yearly for exams, routine tests and overall evaluations. Many veterinarians have special screening programs especially for senior dogs that can include a thorough physical exam; blood test to determine complete blood count; serum biochemistry test, which screens for liver, kidney and blood problems as well as cancer; urinalysis; and dental exams. With these tests, it can be determined whether your dog has any health problems; the results also establish a baseline for your pet against which future test results can be compared.

In addition to these tests, your vet may suggest additional testing, including an EKG, tests for glaucoma and other problems of the eye, chest X-rays, screening for tumors, blood pressure test, test for thyroid function and screening for parasites and reassessment of his preventive program. Your vet also will ask you questions about your dog's diet and activity level, what you feed and the amounts that you feed. This information, along with his evaluation of the dog's overall condition, will enable him to suggest proper dietary changes, if needed.

Veterinarians advise that older dogs need more frequent attention so that any health problems can be detected as early as possible. Serious conditions like kidney disease, heart disease and cancer may not present outward symptoms, or the problem may go undetected if the symptoms are mistaken by owners as just part of the aging process.

Cognitive dysfunction shares much in common with senility and Alzheimer's disease, and dogs are not immune. Dogs can become confused and/or disoriented, lose their house-training, have abnormal sleep-wake cycles and interact differently with their owners. There are many treatment options for dogs with cognitive dysfunction. There is good evidence that continued stimulation in the form of games, play, training and exercise can help to maintain cognitive function. There are also medications (such as seligiline) and antioxidant-fortified senior diets that have been shown to be beneficial.

Cancer is also a condition more common in the elderly. Although lung cancer, which is a major killer in humans, is relatively rare in dogs, almost all of the cancers seen in people are also seen in pets. If pets are getting regular physical examinations, cancers are often detected early. There are a variety of cancer therapies available today, and many pets continue to live happy lives with appropriate treatment.

Degenerative joint disease, often referred to as arthritis, is another malady common to both elderly dogs and humans. A life-time of wear and tear on joints and running around at play eventually takes its toll, resulting in stiffness and difficulty in getting around. Once again, if regular veterinary care has been available, your pet should not have been carrying extra pounds all those years and wearing those joints out before their time. If your pet was unfortunate enough to inherit any of the other developmental orthopedic diseases, battling the onset of degenerative joint disease was probably a longstanding goal. In any case, there are now many effective remedies for managing degenerative joint disease and a number of remarkable surgeries.

Aside from the extra veterinary care, there is much you can do at home to keep your older dog in good condition. The dog's diet is an important factor. If your dog's appetite decreases, he will not be getting the nutrients he needs. He also will lose weight, which is unhealthy for a dog at a proper weight. Conversely, an older dog's metabolism is slower and he usually exercises less, but he should not be allowed to become obese. Obesity in an older dog is especially risky, because extra pounds mean extra stress on the body, increasing his vulnerability to heart disease. Additionally, the extra pounds make it harder for the dog to move about.

You should discuss age-related feeding changes with your vet. For a dog who has lost interest in food, it may be suggested to try some different types of food until you find something new that the dog likes. For an obese dog, a "light"-formula dog food or reducing food portions may be advised, along with exercise appropriate to his physical condition and energy level.

The senior dog should not be allowed to become a "couch potato" despite his old age. He still needs to get up and get moving. Keep up with your daily walks, but keep the distances shorter and let your dog set the pace. If he gets to the point where he's not up for walks, let him stroll around the yard. On the other hand, many dogs remain very active in their senior years, so base changes to the exercise program on your own individual dog and what he's capable of. Don't worry, your Whippet will let you know when it's time to rest.

Keep up with your grooming routine as you always have. Be extra-diligent about checking the skin and coat for problems. Older dogs can experience thinning coats as a normal aging process, but they can also lose hair as a result of medical problems. Some thinning is normal, but patches of baldness or the loss of significant amounts of hair is not.

Hopefully, you've been regular with brushing your dog's teeth

WEATHER WORRIES
Older pets are less tolerant of extremes in weather, both heat and cold. Your older dog should not spend extended periods in the sun; when outdoors in the warm weather, make sure he does not become overheated. In chilly weather, consider a sweater for your dog when outdoors and limit time spent outside. Whether or not his coat is thinning, he will need provisions to keep him warm when the weather is cold. You may even place his bed by a heating duct in your living room or bedroom.

throughout his life. Healthy teeth directly affect overall good health. We already know that bacteria from gum infections can enter the dog's body through the damaged gums and travel to the organs. At a stage in life when his organs don't function as well as they used to, you don't want anything to put additional strain on them. Clean teeth also contribute to a healthy immune system. Offering the dental-type chews in addition to toothbrushing can help, as they remove plaque and tartar as the dog chews.

Along with the same good care you've given him all of his life, pay a little extra attention to your dog in his senior years and keep up with twice-yearly trips to the vet. The sooner a problem is uncovered, the greater the chances of a full recovery.

SHOWING YOUR

WHIPPET

Is dog showing in your blood? Are you excited by the idea of gaiting your handsome Whippet around the ring to the thunderous applause of an enthusiastic audience? Are you certain that your beloved Whippet is flawless? You are not alone! Every loving owner thinks that his dog has no faults, or too few to mention. No matter how many times an owner reads the breed standard, he cannot find any faults in his aristocratic companion dog. If this sounds like you, and if you are considering entering your Whippet in a dog show, here are some basic questions to ask yourself:

- Did you purchase a "show-quality" puppy from the breeder?
- Is your puppy at least six months of age?
- Does the puppy exhibit correct show type for his breed?
- Does your puppy have any disqualifying faults?
- Is your Whippet registered with the American Kennel Club?
- How much time do you have to devote to training, grooming, conditioning and exhibiting your dog?

FOR MORE INFORMATION....

For reliable up-to-date information about registration, dog shows and other canine competitions, contact one of the national registries by mail or via the Internet.

American Kennel Club
5580 Centerview Dr., Raleigh, NC 27606-3390
www.akc.org

United Kennel Club
100 E. Kilgore Road, Kalamazoo, MI 49002
www.ukcdogs.com

Canadian Kennel Club
89 Skyway Ave., Suite 100, Etobicoke, Ontario
M9W 6R4 Canada
www.ckc.ca

The Kennel Club
1-5 Clarges St., Piccadilly, London
W1Y 8AB, UK
www.the-kennel-club.org.uk

- Do you understand the rules and regulations of a dog show?
- Do you have time to learn how to show your dog properly?
- Do you have the financial resources to invest in showing your dog?
- Will you show the dog yourself or hire a professional handler?
- Do you have a vehicle that can accommodate your weekend trips to the dog shows?

Success in the show ring requires more than a pretty face, a waggy tail and a pocketful of liver. Even though dog shows can be exciting and enjoyable, the sport of conformation makes great demands on the exhibitors and the dogs. Winning exhibitors live for their dogs, devoting time and money to their dogs' presentation, conditioning and training. Very few novices, even those with good dogs, will find themselves in the winners' circle, though it does happen. Don't be disheartened, though. Every exhibitor began as a novice and worked his way up to the Group ring. It's the "working your way up" part that you must keep in mind.

Assuming that you have purchased a puppy of the correct type and quality for showing, let's begin to examine the world of showing and what's required to get started. Although the entry fee into a dog show is nominal, there are lots of other hidden costs involved with "finishing" your

Whippet, that is, making him a champion. Things like equipment, travel, training and conditioning all cost money. A more serious campaign will include fees for a professional handler, boarding, cross-country travel and advertising. Top-winning show dogs can represent a very considerable investment—over $100,000 has been spent in campaigning some

Showing your Whippet is both enjoyable and educational. Be a gracious winner or a supportive loser. Showing is about the dogs first!

dogs. (The investment can be less, of course, for owners who don't use professional handlers.)

Many owners, on the other hand, enter their "average" Whippets in dog shows for the fun and enjoyment of it. Dog showing makes an absorbing hobby, with many rewards for dogs and owners alike. If you're having fun, meeting other people who share your interests and enjoying the overall experience, you likely will catch the "bug." Once the dog-show bug bites, its effects can last a lifetime; it's certainly much better than a deer tick! Soon you will be envisioning yourself in the center ring at the Westminster Kennel Club Dog Show in New York City, competing for the prestigious Best in Show cup. This magical dog show is televised annually from Madison Square Garden, and the victorious dog becomes a celebrity overnight.

CONFORMATION SHOWING

Visiting a dog show as a spectator is a great place to start. Pick up the show catalog to find out what time your breed is being shown, who is judging the breed and in which ring the classes will be held. To start, Whippets compete against other Whippets, and the winner is selected as Best of Breed by the judge. This is the procedure for each breed. At a group show, all of the Best of Breed winners go on to compete for Group One in their respective group. For example, all Best of Breed winners in a given group compete against each other; this is done for all seven groups. Finally, all seven group winners go head to head in the ring for the Best in Show award.

What most spectators don't understand is the basic idea of conformation. A dog show is often referred as a "conformation" show. This means that the judge should decide how each dog stacks up (conforms) to the breed standard for his given breed: how well does

> **FIVE CLASSES AT SHOWS**
> At most AKC all-breed shows, there are five regular classes offered: Puppy, Novice, Bred-by-Exhibitor, American-bred and Open. The Puppy Class is usually divided as 6 to 9 months of age and 9 to 12 months of age. When deciding in which class to enter your dog, whether male or female, you must carefully check the show schedule to make sure that you have selected the right class. Depending on the age of the dog, its previous first-place wins and the sex of the dog, you must make the best choice. It is possible to enter a one-year-old dog who has not won sufficient first places in any of the non-Puppy Classes, though the competition is more intense the further you progress from the Puppy Class.

this Whippet conform to the ideal representative detailed in the standard? Ideally, this is what happens. In reality, however, this ideal often gets slighted as the judge compares Whippet #1 to Whippet #2. Again, the ideal is that each dog is judged based on his merits in comparison to his breed standard, not in comparison to the other dogs in the ring. It is easier for judges to compare dogs of the same breed to decide which they think is the better specimen; in the Group and Best in Show ring, however, it is very difficult to compare one breed to another, like apples to oranges. Thus the dog's conformation to the breed standard—not to mention advertising dollars and good handling—is essential to success in conformation shows. The dog described in the standard (the standard for each AKC breed is written and approved by the breed's national parent club and then submitted to the AKC for approval) is the perfect dog of that breed, and breeders keep their eye on the standard when they choose which dogs to breed, hoping to get closer and closer to the ideal with each litter.

Another good first step for the novice is to join a dog club. You will be astonished by the many and different kinds of dog clubs in the country, with about 5,000 clubs holding events every year. Most clubs require that prospective new members present two letters of recommendation from existing members. Perhaps you've

Dog shows are wonderful social events where fanciers and dogs alike can meet and mingle.

made some friends visiting a show held by a particular club and you would like to join that club. Dog clubs may specialize in a single breed, like a local or regional Whippet club, or in a specific pursuit, such as obedience, tracking or hunting tests. There are all-breed clubs for all-dog enthusiasts; they sponsor special training days, seminars on topics like grooming or handling or lectures on breeding or canine genetics. There are also clubs that specialize in certain types of dogs, like sighthounds, hunting dogs, companion dogs, etc.

A parent club is the national organization, sanctioned by the AKC, which promotes and safeguards its breed in the country. The American Whippet Club can be contacted on the Internet at www.americanwhippetclub.net. The parent club holds an annual national specialty show, usually in a different city each year, in which many of the country's top

BECOMING A CHAMPION

An official AKC championship of record requires that a dog accumulate 15 points under three different judges, including two "majors" under different judges. Points are awarded based on the number of dogs entered into competition, varying from breed to breed and place to place. A win of three, four or five points is considered a "major." The AKC annually assigns a schedule of points to adjust for variations that accompany a breed's popularity and the population of a given area.

dogs, handlers and breeders gather to compete. At a specialty show, only members of a single breed are invited to participate. There are also group specialties, in which all members of a group are invited. For more information about dog clubs in your area, contact the AKC at www.akc.org on the Internet or write them at their Raleigh, NC address.

OBEDIENCE TRIALS
Any dog registered with the AKC, regardless of neutering or other disqualifications that would preclude entry in conformation competition, can participate in obedience trials.

There are three levels of difficulty in obedience competition. The first (and easiest) level is the Novice, in which dogs can earn the Companion Dog (CD) title. The intermediate level is the Open level, in which the Companion Dog Excellent (CDX) title is awarded. The advanced level is the Utility level, in which dogs compete for the Utility Dog (UD) title. Classes at each level are further divided into "A" and "B," with "A" for beginners and "B" for those with more experience. In order to win a title at a given level, a dog must earn three "legs." A "leg" is accomplished when a dog scores 170 or higher (200 is a perfect score). The scoring system gets a little trickier when you understand that a dog

must score more than 50% of the points available for each exercise in order to actually earn the points. Available points for each exercise range between 20 and 40.

A dog must complete different exercises at each level of obedience. The Novice exercises are the easiest, with the Open and finally the Utility levels progressing in difficulty. Examples of Novice exercises are on- and off-lead heeling, a figure-8 pattern, performing a recall (or come), long sit and long down and standing for examination. In the Open level, the Novice-level exercises are required again, but this time without a leash and for longer durations. In addition, the dog must clear a broad jump, retrieve over a jump and drop on recall. In the Utility level, the exercises are quite difficult, including executing basic commands based on hand signals, following a complex heeling pattern, locating articles based on scent discrimination and completing jumps at the handler's direction.

Once he's earned the UD title,

AKC GROUPS
For showing purposes, the American Kennel Club divides its recognized breeds into seven groups: Hounds, Sporting Dogs, Working Dogs, Terriers, Toys, Non-Sporting Dogs and Herding Dogs. The Whippet competes in the Hound Group.

a dog can go on to win the prestigious title of Utility Dog Excellent (UDX) by winning "legs" in ten shows. Additionally, Utility Dogs who win "legs" in Open B and Utility B earn points toward the lofty title of Obedience Trial Champion (OTCh.). Established in 1977 by the AKC, this title requires a dog to earn 100 points as well as three first places in a combination of Open B and Utility B classes under three different judges. The "brass ring" of obedience competition is the AKC's National Obedience Invitational. This is an exclusive competition for only the cream of the obedience crop. In order to qualify for the invitational, a dog must be ranked in either the top 25 all-breeds in obedience or in the top three for his breed in obedience. The title at stake here is that of National Obedience Champion (NOC).

Winning in the show ring acknowledges the success of the dog and everyone involved with them.

AGILITY TRIALS

Agility trials became sanctioned by the AKC in August 1994, when the first licensed agility trials were held. Since that time, agility certainly has grown in popularity by leaps and bounds, literally! The AKC allows all registered breeds (including Miscellaneous Class breeds) to participate, providing the dog is 12 months of age or older. Agility is designed so that the handler demonstrates how well the dog can work at his side. The handler directs his dog through, over, under and around an obstacle course that includes jumps, tires, the dog walk, weave poles, pipe tunnels, collapsed tunnels and more. While working his way through the course, the dog must keep one eye and ear on the handler and the rest of his body on the course. The handler runs along with the dog, giving verbal and hand signals to guide the dog through the course.

The first organization to promote agility trials in the US was the United States Dog Agility Association, Inc. (USDAA). Established in 1986, the USDAA sparked the formation of many member clubs around the country. To participate in USDAA trials, dogs must be at least 18 months of age. The USDAA and AKC both offer titles to winning dogs, although the exercises and requirements of the two organizations differ.

TRACKING

Tracking tests are exciting ways to test your Whippet's instinctive scenting ability on a competitive level. All dogs have a nose, and all breeds are welcome in tracking tests. The first AKC-licensed tracking test took place in 1937 as part of the Utility level at an obedience trial, and thus competitive tracking was officially begun. The first title, Tracking Dog (TD), was offered in 1947, ten years after the first official tracking test. It was not until 1980 that the AKC added the title Tracking Dog Excellent (TDX), which was followed by the title Versatile Surface Tracking (VST) in 1995. Champion Tracker (CT) is awarded to a dog who has earned all three of those titles.

LURE COURSING

Owners of sighthound breeds have the opportunity to participate in lure coursing. Lure-coursing events are exciting and

---

RACING WHIPPETS

Whippet racing is not affiliated with gambling; rather, it is to assess the dogs' speed and award titles to winners. An artificial lure is used to incite the hounds, and the dogs must race the course without interfering with other dogs.

There are several organizations that sponsor and regulate racing just for Whippets. For straight racing, these include the Whippet Racing Association (WRA), the North American Whippet Racing Association (NAWRA) and the Continental Whippet Alliance (CWA). For oval racing, Whippets can participate in races held by the National Oval Track Racing Association (NOTRA), which sponsors races for most of the sighthound breeds.

Whippets of all abilities can compete and enjoy racing, as the grading system allow dogs to compete against others of similar skill. It is wise to look into the requirements of each club before deciding with which club to become involved with your Whippet. Contact these organizations for more information and to find one of their local clubs to help you get started:

WRA: www.whippetracing.org
NAWRA: www.nawra.com
CWA: www.continentalwhippetalliance.org
NOTRA: www.notra.org

Whippet races, unlike professional Greyhound races, serve to award the dogs titles instead of the owners cash prizes.

fast-paced, requiring dogs to follow an artificial lure around a course on an open field. Scores are based on the dog's speed, enthusiasm, agility, endurance and ability to follow the lure. At the non-competitive level, lure coursing is designed to gauge a sighthound's instinctive coursing ability. Competitive lure coursing is more demanding, requiring training and conditioning for a dog to develop his coursing instincts and skills to the fullest, thus preserving the intended function of all sighthound breeds. Breeds eligible for AKC lure coursing are the Whippet, Basenji, Greyhound, Italian Greyhound, Afghan Hound, Borzoi, Ibizan Hound, Pharaoh Hound, Irish Wolfhound, Scottish Deerhound, Saluki and Rhodesian Ridgeback.

Lure coursing on a competitive level is certainly wonderful physical and mental exercise for a dog. A dog must be at least one year of age to enter an AKC coursing event, and he must not have any disqualifications according to his breed standard. Check the AKC's rules and regulations for details. To get started, you can consult the AKC's website to help you find a coursing club in your area. A club can introduce you to the sport and help you learn how to train your dog correctly.

Sighthounds also can participate in events sponsored by the American Sighthound Field Association (ASFA), an organization devoted to the pursuit of lure coursing. The ASFA was founded in 1972 as a means of keeping open field coursing dogs fit in the off-season. It has grown into the largest lure-coursing association in the world. Dogs must be of an accepted sighthound breed in order to be eligible for participation. Each dog must pass a certification run in which he shows that he can run with another dog without interfering.

Coursing is an all-day event, held in all weather conditions. It is great fun for the whole family, but on a rainy, cold day, it's best to leave the kids at home.

Once bitten by the racing bug, enthusiasts make these outings every-weekend affairs. It's hard to beat the fun and the excitement of Whippet racing!

INDEX

My Whippet

PUT YOUR PUPPY'S FIRST PICTURE HERE

Dog's Name _____

Date _____ Photographer _____